I AM THE STORY

HUMAN HORIZONS SERIES

I AM THE STORY

The Art of Puppetry in Education and Therapy

Caroline Astell-Burt

A Condor Book
Souvenir Press (E&A) Ltd

Contents

Acknowledgements

I wish to thank staff and students from all years of the London School of Puppetry who have enabled me to develop my ideas about the teaching of puppetry. Barry Camp for his practical help as our external examiner; Wendy Cook who has made such an exciting breakthrough for me in the exploration and teaching of puppet movement. Ronnie Le Drew for his wonderful puppetry performances; my colleagues and some of the contributors to the London School of Puppetry Conferences: Maureen McGough; Sue Speechley; Ann Campion; Carol Armstrong; Bjorg Mykle; Mickey Aronoff; Meena Naik; Sidsel Berg; Dr Santiranjan Paul; Gary Friedman; Madge Bray; Aileen Finlay.

Maggie and Steph; Dr. Barnardos; Mencap; the Ryegate Centre, Sheffield; the Geoffrey Ost Award, Sheffield University; Henshaws School; Shipley Toy and Leisure Library; the Goldhay Group, Peterborough.

The works of Meyer Contractor; Nancy Cole; Henryk Jurkowski; Aaron Copeland. National Youth Music Theatre; Royal Opera House; Oxford Playhouse; Little Angel Marionette Theatre; Bolton Octagon; the actor/director Wilfred Harrison; Over the Top Puppet Company; Bread and Puppet Theatre; Richard Robinson and his Oggle Oggle Box; Horse and Bamboo.

The children or students and staff of Highbury Quadrant School, Islington; Harborne School, Islington; Primrose Montessori School, Islington; Rosemary School, Islington; Gargrave and Threshfield Schools, North Yorkshire.

Jenny Baynes for extending my reading and learning capacity; Ray and Joan Da Silva for puppet books.

I wish to thank my parents for their practical support and perhaps most of all my own children John-Philip and Elizabeth.

Preface

At the time of writing the first edition of this book twenty years ago, I was a residential social worker for Dr Barnardo's. It was usual to let the older girls stay up if there was something of particular interest on television. The two girls I have in mind were close friends and had been at Barnardo's from being tiny babies—one had been disabled by the thalidomide drug, the other had spina bifida and hydrocephalus. They were excited because their consultant paediatrician was going to be on the box talking about disabled children. From the television in the corner the doctor said that he thought it might be better to allow newborn babies with disabilities to be left to die. The two girls looked at each other in disbelief: 'He's talking about us,' they said to each other. They were a pair of fairly typical teenagers. What about their stories, their potential? Are we supposed to regard them both as irrelevancies?

At about that time I went to a large paediatric teaching hospital to give a lunchtime talk in the postgraduate centre. I was showing slides and talking about some of my work with people with severe learning disabilities when a young doctor interrupted in amazement: 'So they are capable of giving and receiving love.' Let them tell their own story and you would know, I thought.

At another hospital—a long-stay hospital for people with learning disabilities—I was performing in a men's ward. I went around showing the puppets, working closely with each man. The nurses hung around the edges of the group—one smoking a cigarette out of the open window—another told me not to bother with one man because he was blind. He had no significance for them and no story.

The opening of the London School of Puppetry fulfilled our vision to develop a professional training in puppetry to include teaching puppeteers to work in special needs of all kinds. The school also hosted several international conferences on the use of puppetry in education and therapy: these have brought specialists from all over the world to share their experiences of puppetry as a vital creative force.

What we all have in common is our belief, backed by practical experience, that the puppet can give those without a voice not only their voice but their story. Bjorg Mykle, from Norway, working with suspected sexually abused children made four puppets she called her 'assistants'. These puppets were extremely attractive with woolly sweaters, denim dungarees, dark faces, round noses and curly dark hair but no mouths. The mouth was to be added by the child when she was ready to tell her story.

Mickey Aronoff, play therapist and social worker in the USA, who uses puppets in her work with children in hospital, refers to the way puppets 'speak' for the 'frozen voice', as she so aptly describes it.

While working on a shadow puppet workshop with a group of adults with learning disabilities I made a shadow of a house—the idea was that each member of the group should put a puppet into the house and tell us about it. I asked one of them to tell his story—'I am the story' was the dignified reply.

Introduction

Twenty years ago, my work was new. Now, I am delighted that I am one of many people committed to developing the creativity of all individuals with or without disabilities who together make up our community. It goes without saying that without the arts and artists our scientific and technological culture could not exist. A challenging, creative, communicative community offers a better and more successful educational experience.

Creative expression gives coherence—personal coherence—to the individual, even when their relationship to the outside world may be confused, or apparently irrelevant. Art particularises who we are as individuals and how we form relationships. It provides the imagery in which we wrap up our ideas and convictions to present to others, making experience concrete and available for sharing. It gives us the coherence we need to be understood by others, and indeed to understand ourselves better. Art cannot exist without us holding convictions, but at the same time it enables us to hold those convictions. Does this apply to anyone, however? The answer has to be yes, because to have a view is to be human—it is the story of that person. Many languages of artistic expression make up our culture.

Twenty years ago I remember the public debate questioning the creativity of a disabled person. This book was then, and is still, dedicated to a young man, Warwick Stephenson, who has a life and a story, even though he needs to be surrounded by many patient carers who believe that he has indeed a life worth living. The healing and

Fig. 1.

educative presence of the listener, the companion within the creative context, cannot be underestimated.

The predicament of dependency of the person with obvious disabilities is not so different from the situation of the whole of society. We are not in control, however much we like to pretend so, but are vulnerable to natural disaster, accident etc. The creative community is our only defence.

The Elizabethan philosopher, Francis Bacon, advised that 'the Fall' (the loss of innocence and loss of dominion over nature) could in part be remedied by education and therapy (through the study of science and art). Heinrich von Kleist uses the marionette to describe our dilemma as fallen gravity-bound beings. Through puppetry, we can work without our fatal ego interfering with our creativity and cutting us off from our audience.

Was it Leonard Cohen the poet and songwriter who talked about art as the only kind of expression that can heal? Essentially, the kind of healing I am talking about is the desperate aloneness of being shut in with illness, incapacity and disability, resulting in self-centredness and any kind of relationship being compromised.

The artist Oscar Schlemmer, in his notes after the performance of his marionette Triadic Ballet, writes that egoism and 'dualistic contrast are transcended to give way to the collective'. The creative environment has to be affirming and fearless, or else it is absurd and meaningless. Aaron Copeland in 'Music and the Imagination' once again emphasises the creative community:

You cannot make art out of fear and suspicion; you can only make it out of affirmative beliefs. This sense of affirmation can be had only in part from one's inner being; for the rest it must be continually reactivated by a creative and yea-saying atmosphere in the life about one. The artist should feel himself affirmed and buoyed up by his community. In other words, art and the life of art must

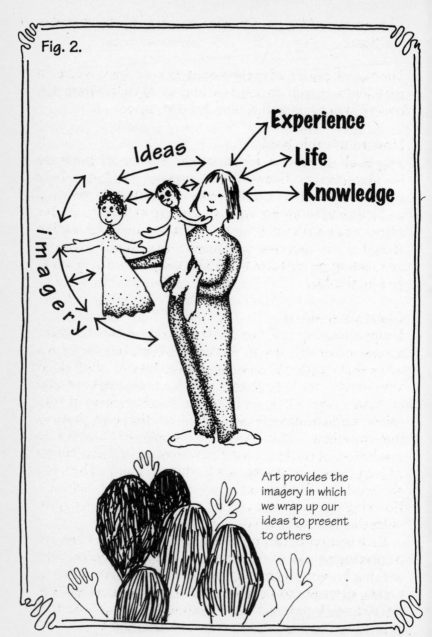

Fig. 2.

Ideas

Experience

Life

Knowledge

imagery

Art provides the imagery in which we wrap up our ideas to present to others

mean something, in the deepest sense, to the everyday citizen.

The social aspect of puppetry is one of huge value in enabling a person to express him or herself within the society about him and to find his own place.

How to use this book

This book is a manual for those who wish to use puppetry in education or therapy. The original brief has been expanded to include special needs of all kinds. I have used a client-centred approach that will accommodate people with learning disabilities. Your aim as artist or teacher should be to understand how and why puppetry works, and then to be sensitive to the disability in order to adapt and be flexible.

Client-centredness

I might, once upon a time, have made an issue out of the specific needs of a person with disabilities, but over years of working with all kinds of people, I have found those with disabilities have often been the most charming and amenable (and sometimes not), while those who are so-called 'normal' have occasionally been the most obstructive, dishonest and hardest to work with by far. So I do not believe there is a need to distinguish between clients as long as you keep your work 'client-centred'. Then you are working flexibly off their responses and interests. Knowing that there is someone there, ready to listen, provides the best positive encouragement.

Each section of this book includes exercises designed to be developmental, so that you are able to progress through the book with increasing understanding. At different points, descriptions or references to new projects and significant work are included to show the possibilities that exist for using puppetry in education and therapy.

Section 1 The chapters on 'your vocabulary' will suggest a particular range of basic puppet types which I recommend for the job. These can be simply designed and made.

Basic exercises introduce the puppets and their essential qualities. Some of these exercises need to be done with other people, and would also be appropriate for your clients. Descriptions are given of different stages, booths and tables that would be appropriate, followed by simple exercises to accustom you to these performance spaces.

Section 2 explores the nature of storytelling through puppet theatre—the history of puppet theatre, what its therapeutic value is, and how to achieve it. Larger collaborative projects are included.

Section 3 consists of a detailed description of the puppet as a surrogate object, with exercises to open up this idea. Essentially, the puppet stands instead of the individual, enabling him/her to become safely and personally involved with such issues as prostitution, political freedom or child abuse.

Section 4 examines spoken language and communication, and covers a very varied range of material, such as literacy work for young mainstream children, autism, and various projects for people with learning disabilities.

Section 5 reviews the original 'I am the story' projects and considers some difficulties in including puppetry in educational or therapeutic programmes. The book ends in the audience of a puppet show.

Section 1

The right puppet for the right job
Your vocabulary
Glove/hand puppetry
Rod puppetry
Shadow puppetry
Marionettes
Stages, booths and tables

The right puppet for the right job

To enable someone to tell their story, having the 'right tools for the job' is essential. But learning skills and techniques, such as those attached to a particular puppet type, might in fact mask personal expression and obscure genuine impulse. There is no point pushing glove puppets, for example, at someone because they are your favourite medium—puppetry is a wide and varied art form, and experts in it should know the benefits that are provided by the range and type of puppets available nationally and internationally.

We all need to achieve a balance between skills acquisition for its own sake and truthful, unaffected, personal expression that is a far more delicate flower. And so the term 'tools' refers to a whole range of qualities you need for this work. Practical puppetry, knowledge and understanding of disability, wisdom, and flexibility to adapt to the needs of any individual or group: all those are essential requirements.

> Our guiding principle is the impulse in every human being to respond to objects as if they are alive (whether by operating them themselves or by participating as a spectator).

The kind of puppet chosen is based on how you present the puppets to enable an individual to externalise or give physical reality to an internal, imagined image. Working closely with your clients, there are three ways:

3

1. *A puppet-making session: two alternatives*

By preparing the technical aspects of the puppet in advance (so that the puppets do not actually fall apart), and providing the clients (of any age) with suitable structures or surfaces to complete, the process of making might be valuably explored. See figure 3 for instant puppets or use any of the other puppet-making methods described in this book.

For many years there has been a fashion for junk puppets. Puppeteers or teachers do a short workshop and junk rod puppets made from a variety of wooden spoons, paper plates, egg boxes and yoghurt pots are the result. However, be warned: they fall apart quite easily.

2. *You can play to the client or group*

In this case there is no limit to the type of puppet you use from your own collection. In order to encourage the best possible practice, you need to be able to work most puppets and to have with you an exciting and stimulating collection for performance. London School of Puppetry students have several five minute performances they use as a starting point.

3. *The client group can play with puppets immediately, for and with each other*

Found objects, such as dolls or any other toys, as well as puppets, might also elicit a 'play response' in your clients. Exercises to start off puppet activity can be found throughout this book.

Thus when choosing the right puppets for the right job, be wary of using puppets which become obstacles to creativity. Any puppet can be a medium for imitating and characterising human expression and, in response to it, we invest the object of our desires with energy and action. You need to gauge what technical skills are required. Ease of manipulation (from 'very easy', when operating puppets for the less able, to 'challenging', for someone gifted) might

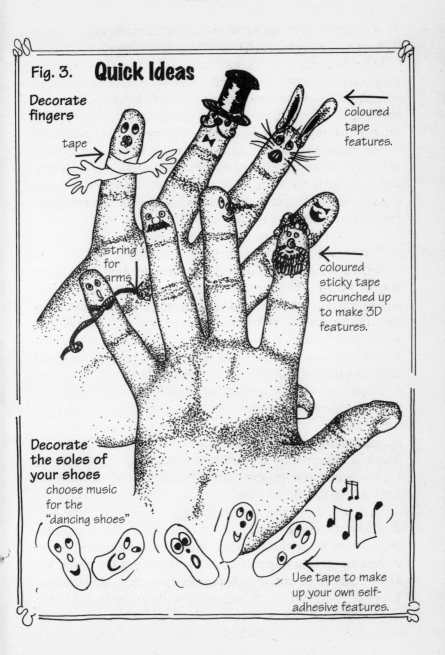

Fig. 3. **Quick Ideas**

Decorate fingers

tape

coloured tape features.

string for arms

coloured sticky tape scrunched up to make 3D features.

Decorate the soles of your shoes

choose music for the "dancing shoes"

Use tape to make up your own self-adhesive features.

still produce a response which, although resulting from new-found knowledge has a counterfeit quality.

In education, there is, however, a tendency to use puppetry as a means to another end—perhaps as a visual aid—as mindless as playing a violin for arm exercises. If we are looking at puppetry as a language for those with less of a voice than most of us, then we need to pay more attention to the thought behind the action than to the mechanical action itself and craft technique. Ultimately, the point of the activity is to bring about communication, a sharing. Despite its robust folk origins as a performance art, puppetry is curiously associated with childhood, when, in fact, it is a superb art form for any age—it is both visual art/sculpture and performance.

It has specific disciplines and techniques that need to be learnt. It requires time and commitment. It is a vital art, it has the potential to move or horrify. In the hands of meaningful artists, it will be distinguished by its relevance, by its power, and not as a consolation or refuge—but by its sheer appropriateness as a medium for the least or most able to express themselves.

There are certain practical considerations that affect what puppets we use:

1. *Suitability of surroundings*
Shadow puppets need darkness. Table-top puppets need tables. Some rod puppets need height; some marionettes need space for suspension.

2. *Physical challenges*
Can someone without hands manipulate puppets? Some people operating puppets want to hide from the audience. How easily can you adapt puppet objects and stages for use?

3. Physical and psychological demands

Different types of puppets make different kinds of physical and psychological demands on your clients. Can you assess which puppets would be the most appropriate? See Fig. 4.

Assuming you do have a good range of puppet types the following checklist could be useful to assess creative thinking in your client. See Fig. 5.

Checklist

1. What kind of relationship does your client have with the puppet—is s/he engaged as a spectator or as a puppet operator?
2. Once engaged in either role, is there a desire to give in to social expectations to respond to the audience or to the puppets?
3. Is there a clear desire to use the puppet to communicate to spectators?
4. Is there the ability to distinguish between doll play which does not need an audience, and puppet play which does?
5. Are puppets being used to extend social repertoire to communicate? (In intellectual content, expression of feelings; making moral choices).
6. How appropriate is the action for the character depicted by the puppet—this might be play with archetypes: good, bad, king, queen, witch etc.
7. Is your client able to play jokes with the puppets—to play with the ridiculous, the unexpected or the incongruous.

Fig. 4.
Contact and control of the puppets . .

The more contact usually the more direct communication.
A puppet's physical closeness to the puppeteer displays the person's readiness to make direct communication with others.

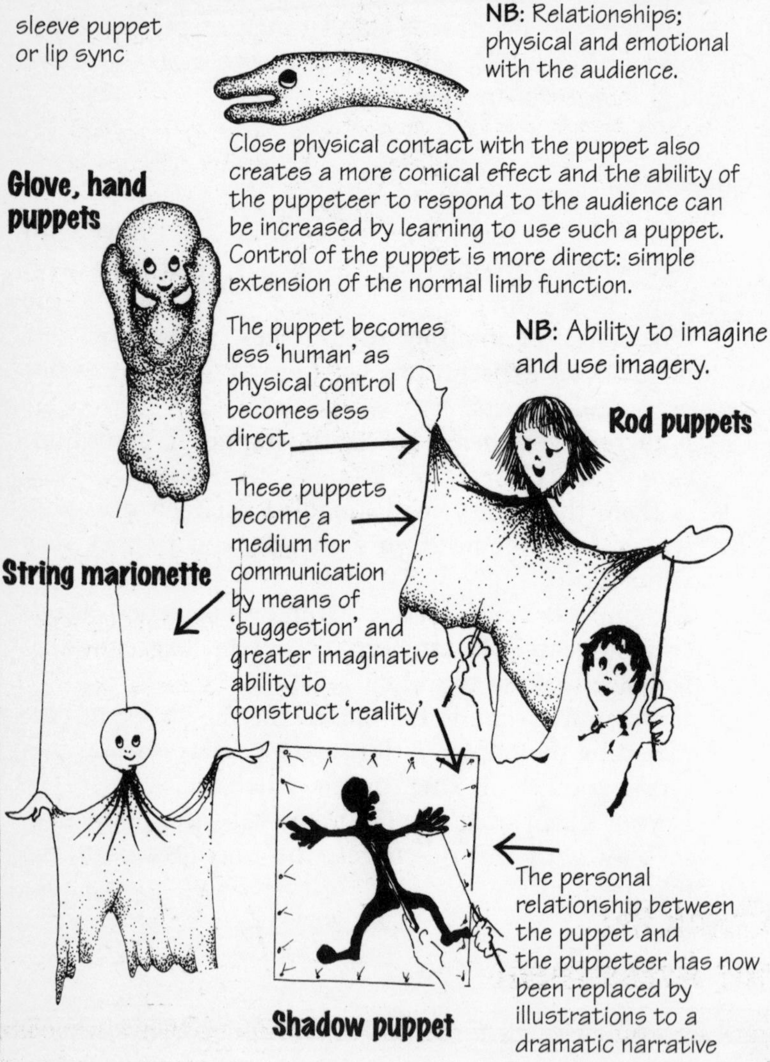

sleeve puppet
or lip sync

NB: Relationships;
physical and emotional
with the audience.

Glove, hand puppets

Close physical contact with the puppet also
creates a more comical effect and the ability of
the puppeteer to respond to the audience can
be increased by learning to use such a puppet.
Control of the puppet is more direct: simple
extension of the normal limb function.

The puppet becomes
less 'human' as
physical control
becomes less
direct

NB: Ability to imagine
and use imagery.

Rod puppets

These puppets
become a
medium for
communication
by means of
'suggestion' and
greater imaginative
ability to
construct 'reality'

String marionette

The personal
relationship between
the puppet and
the puppeteer has now
been replaced by
illustrations to a
dramatic narrative

Shadow puppet

Fig. 5.

Check list for Assessment

Your vocabulary

'The soul of the puppet is in the palm of the hand.'
Sergei Obraztov

Puppetry is a language—and it consists of signs, symbols and meanings universally understood. It is interesting that when I have taught students at the London School of Puppetry, under pressure they make a grab at an idea in order to get started on a piece of work. If instinctively they discover something that turns out to be meaningful, then their hand really does become the soul of the puppet, with layers of personal meaning, but, on the other hand, if the idea is nothing more than a superficial bit of puppet action, then their link with the puppet will never be cemented as part of their language.

Essentially, puppetry is a language of *movement*. This often surprises those of my students who want to get straight into *talking* with puppets. But if movement is not your starting point, then you end up with puppets as talking heads with no interesting action. When you pick up a puppet, play with it to find out what actions it does. Every puppet is different and even ones apparently quite similar will do some actions better than others. When you design a puppet, before you make it, it is worth thinking about the kind of character you want and how the character will reveal itself in movement.

Working with our choreographer, Wendy Cook, we explored the design of a puppet related to the movement it has to do. She built her work with puppeteers on the movement principles of Rudolph Laban. She asked us to consider the following basic structural factors which influence movement. (She has set up exercises for a London

School of Puppetry class to imagine we are a particular shape and to move in the way the shape demands.)

- The up-down aspects of a puppet that make it seem *pin-like*.
- The left to right symmetry of a figure that make it appear *wall-like*.
- The curling, circling, enclosing aspects of a figure that make it appear *ball-like*.
- The twist between parts of the figure which make it seem *screw-like*.

An example might be to think of the story of Red Riding Hood. You are planning your production—and start to think about how you are going to make the puppets.

Red Riding Hood: perhaps ball-like—she is holding her basket—enclosing the basket—perhaps protecting it from the Wolf—she picks flowers. Does she need to be a glove puppet, therefore?

The Wolf: he darts around hiding behind trees, he is unpredictable, twisting this way and that, appearing and disappearing. He needs to have a moving mouth, but all the rest of the movement is in his trunk. Could he be a mouth puppet with screw-like characteristics?

The Grandmother: in order to get the contrast—you might think of making her pin-like. Very upright, nervously awaiting her grandchild, moving around her room, getting into bed, out of bed, standing up, sitting down. Plenty of potential for the Wolf to wind himself around her—before dressed in her bonnet, he gets into bed. Could she be a rod puppet?

The Woodcutter: wall-like, he peers in through the window—a big, comforting presence—moving from side to side, cutting off the escape of the Wolf before cutting him open! Could he be a wall-like puppet?

Before you start to make puppets you *always* need to

think about them in terms of movement. Speech will come out of that movement but at a much later stage.

I have included only a small range of puppets for you to make to start you creating your vocabulary. Figs 16a–e represent a variety of ways to make essential features. I would suggest you make any one of the puppets, as a means of acquainting yourself with each generic type. This is not a book on puppet making, but a guide to take you through the basic principles to enable you to develop your own personal understanding of the art form. Normally, when teaching, this section of the book would represent one day's work.

For each puppet type, there is a short project on how to make these, followed by exercises on playing with them. It would be best to work in a group, training together, because you always need an outside eye—your perspective on the puppet is working from behind and often below or above—you need the guidance of your 'director' to help you at all times. Puppetry is very physical and tiring, you will need plenty of breaks, so that is when you become the spectator. As so many clients will spend more time in the audience than operating, it is as important to understand their perspective as to understand how to operate the puppets.

Glove/hand puppetry

I am starting with the glove or hand puppet—for no particular reason other than it is often the first type we encounter as children. Although it is an excellent puppet for an audience with any type of disability to watch, these puppets also pose the greatest threat to the successful therapeutic process when it comes to client use. The physical proximity to the puppet demands too much commitment from the client in the formal session. If these puppets are left available, then it is best to observe whether they are picked up and played with as dolls, before you ask the client to use them in your presence.

The second type of puppet is illustrated in Fig. 7. This is called a moving mouth puppet or lip-sync puppet—boys, and teenagers particularly, like the latter. There is the challenge for them in the obvious technical synchronising skills required.

When you have made a head (see Fig. 6), it is soft, easy and light to handle leaving your hand free to pick up props. The features of the design are very important to note for the reasons which follow.

Some people will not put their hands inside a glove puppet. They watch their hands disappearing up the bottom of perhaps a crocodile, or Mister Punch's dog Toby, and it frightens them—which is hardly surprising. With the design in Fig. 6 their hand is always visible. You can go on later to a glove puppet that covers the hand (Fig. 8). I sometimes use clear plastic gloves or make polythene mittens, followed by organza, then muslin, then cotton and so on, so that the hand disappears in stages. By then you will have achieved a maturity in object continuity and be able to proceed more or less as normal after a few weeks.

The traditional glove puppet more or less fixes the character. When using the recommended design, make a collection of interesting gloves—woolly, rubber, sparkly, fingerless—put these on with the head and note how the character changes.

The traditional glove puppet enclosing the whole hand in cloth can frustrate the picking up of props for someone with small or weak hands. In this design the hand can be left free. Glove or hand puppets are *the* puppets for picking up props. This is the best way to use them—for counting, carrying, giving, taking, sorting, hammering.

Simple Glove Head

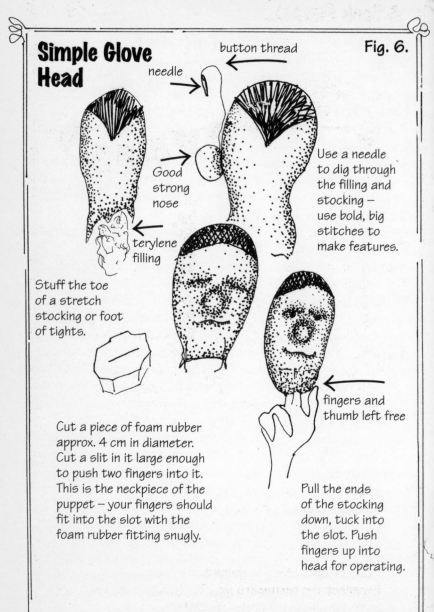

button thread

needle

Fig. 6.

Good strong nose

terylene filling

Use a needle to dig through the filling and stocking – use bold, big stitches to make features.

Stuff the toe of a stretch stocking or foot of tights.

fingers and thumb left free

Cut a piece of foam rubber approx. 4 cm in diameter. Cut a slit in it large enough to push two fingers into it. This is the neckpiece of the puppet – your fingers should fit into the slot with the foam rubber fitting snugly.

Pull the ends of the stocking down, tuck into the slot. Push fingers up into head for operating.

14

A Sock Puppet...

Fig. 7.

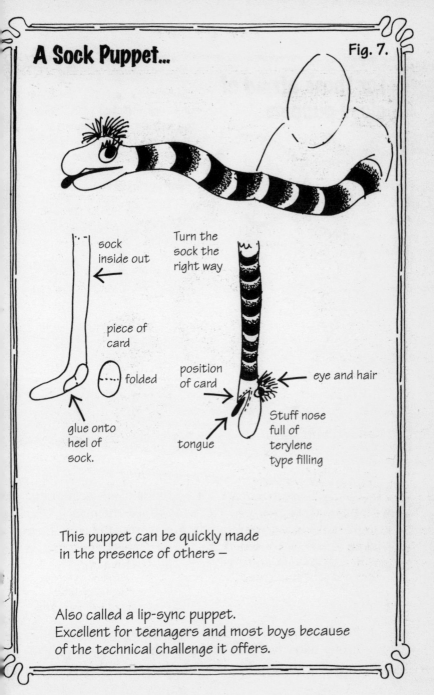

sock
inside out

Turn the
sock the
right way

piece of
card

···· folded

position
of card

eye and hair

glue onto
heel of
sock.

tongue

Stuff nose
full of
terylene
type filling

This puppet can be quickly made
in the presence of others –

Also called a lip-sync puppet.
Excellent for teenagers and most boys because
of the technical challenge it offers.

15

For those afraid of glove puppets

Fig. 8.

Simple clear polythene mitten machine stitched with drawn-on features — The puppeteer's hand can be seen clearly — Other mittens may be made of organza, chiffon or net. Features need to be very striking.

The following exercises are for you to get well acquainted with puppets, so that you are ready to use them with your group: make sure your hands are warm and you have shaken them to loosen them up, stretched your fingers gently side to side and forwards and backwards.

Exercises

1 Put head on to first and second finger. It should fit firmly with the foam rubber in the neck-piece providing enough grip for you to move your fingers from

16

side to side and up and down. Move your fingers around so that they become as flexible as possible. Change hands and repeat.

2 Use the other hand to support the puppet-arm at the elbow, bounce the arm up and down and feel the weight of the puppet—gravity is important, as it gives reality to the puppet. For example, if the puppet is sad it will need to look heavy, and when happy it will need to look light, but you can't have the contrast in movement without being aware of the weight at all times. Change arms and repeat.

3 Flop the puppet forward—your wrist becomes its waist and the back of the wrist the puppet's bottom. (Most commercial glove puppets finish at the wrist— but in doing so lose much potential. When you make a full glove puppet the cloth of the glove should go down to your elbow). Exercise the joint, change hands and repeat.

4 Now put the puppet to sleep in the crook of your arm like a baby. Snuggle it face down so that the eyes are not showing (glove puppets always sleep facing away from the audience, otherwise they look dead). Simulate breathing by very slightly lifting the waist of the puppet in time with your own breath. Feel the weight of the puppet—the puppet arm must be completely relaxed.

5 When the puppet has been asleep for a bit, let it wake up very slowly, sit up, look around and notice some-thing or someone nearby, look again, rub its eyes and then wave. Make sure the getting up happens in stages and don't forget about the weight of the puppet. Change arms, go back to the beginning of 4 and repeat.

That was a sequence of simple actions to learn step by step. If you have a group that is excitable, then ask them

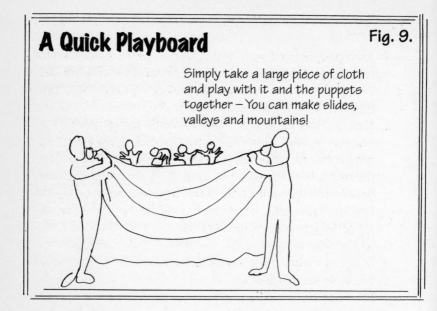

A Quick Playboard

Fig. 9.

Simply take a large piece of cloth and play with it and the puppets together – You can make slides, valleys and mountains!

to take the puppets and put them all to sleep. It works wonders!

Exercises

In a group, go through the wake-up sequence, but end up with the puppets doing four distinct actions:

1 They see each other
2 They wave
3 They see another puppet
4 They wave.

Gradually you will be enabling your group to work in sequences, rather than in random, thoughtless actions that will eventually bore them.

18

Exercises

1 Two people hold up a large cloth to make a playboard for the puppets to walk along. Everyone else should watch until their turn comes either to hold the cloth or to walk the puppet. (See Fig. 9).

2 One person at a time should walk the puppet at a normal speed along the playboard—remembering where the feet should be. Make sure the eyes of the puppet are looking, because it is the eyeline that makes the puppet look alive and intelligent. Carry this out with the puppet playing *'happy'*. Count to three between each movement.

3 Make the puppet *pause*, *look* where it is going.

4 Make it *look* out at the audience.

5 Make it *see* someone.

6 Wave at the person it *sees*.

7 Make it look around to where it is supposed to be going.

8 Make it walk off *looking* the way it is going.

9 Change the puppet to the other hand and repeat. Make the puppet *'sad'* this time. Repeat this, doing a variety of moods.

10 With two people holding up the cloth, and others watching and taking turns, have four puppeteers put their puppets up on to the playboard to await their turn.

   • The first puppet holds a prop—a baby's large cloth brick is good—not something shiny.
   • The next puppet looks at it from a distance very carefully—are the eyes of the puppet fixed on to the object?

11 Pass the object along the line from one puppet to another and then back along again to the beginning.

12 Use vocal sounds to suggest to the spectators exactly
    how heavy this object is.
13 Choose three significant moments in a fairy story and
    put each one into tableau format and freeze.
14 Finally, choose a very simple fairy story and tell it
    with a narrator (no need for the puppets to speak).
    Use anything for props and costumes; use your own
    bodies for scenery, etc., and allow any character to
    play the parts. You have five minutes to tell the whole
    story—but rather than have continuous movement,
    use the tableau technique and freeze.

Maurice Mouse (Fig. 10) and the miniature walking
puppet (Fig. 11) are further examples of hand puppets.
Maurice Mouse should be treated like any glove puppet
so you can use the exercises above for him. The miniature
walking hand puppet is a very sweet, very comical figure.
I have included some exercises to start you off. This is an
example of a puppet type that is completely irresistible!

Think of puppetry as a visual art—a series of frames in
a stop frame animation film. You need the least possible movement in order to strike up the next gesture.
Think of it as making a series of good photographs.

Exercises

1 Everyone, one at a time, climb their puppets up on
  to the table very slowly, as if they were shy.
2 Shuffle them together into a line to dance the can-can.
  (Puppeteers will need to squash up together.)
3 One puppet steps forward as if it had seen something,
  then all the other puppets cluster around to have a

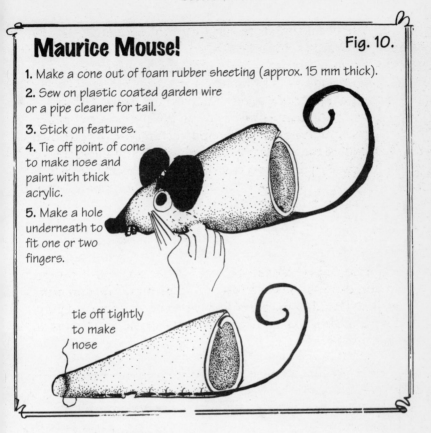

Maurice Mouse!

Fig. 10.

1. Make a cone out of foam rubber sheeting (approx. 15 mm thick).

2. Sew on plastic coated garden wire or a pipe cleaner for tail.

3. Stick on features.

4. Tie off point of cone to make nose and paint with thick acrylic.

5. Make a hole underneath to fit one or two fingers.

tie off tightly
to make
nose

look too. Allow all the puppets to repeat the action.

4 Make a rough little ball out of masking tape (so that it doesn't roll away) and use the little puppets to play a game of football.

Glove puppets, out of use, can look quite unattractive, as, obviously, they collapse when there is no hand inside them. If you are working with people who are not highly motivated, it is sometimes a good idea to make your puppets so that they have some support such as quilting to give them bulk when not in use (see Fig. 12). It is also

Fig. 11.

These puppets need a table-top to walk on

10 cm

7 cm

Back view of piece of foam (a bath sponge)

Cut slit to put forefinger (2nd) and 3rd finger through to make the legs

important in your puppetry design that the puppets have strong clear features.

For many years I worked with large glove puppets that were drawn, cuddled and invited for tea, and were rarely operated as normal glove puppets by my clients. I question the use of this kind of puppet as a first puppet, because they require excellent hand function in order to make them work, and adults with learning or some physical disabilities frequently do not have this; furthermore, as far as the hands of small children are concerned, puppets have to be too small to be dramatically effective.

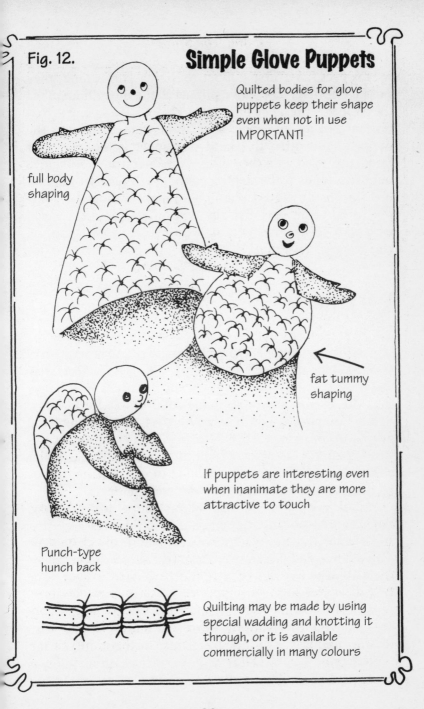

Fig. 12.

Simple Glove Puppets

Quilted bodies for glove
puppets keep their shape
even when not in use
IMPORTANT!

full body
shaping

fat tummy
shaping

If puppets are interesting even
when inanimate they are more
attractive to touch

Punch-type
hunch back

Quilting may be made by using
special wadding and knotting it
through, or it is available
commercially in many colours

23

However, as a first puppet to watch performing, they can be effective. The glove puppet is the most 'human' of the puppet genres. For this reason they elicit a strong verbal response in an audience: spectators want to talk to the puppets, and often this kind of puppet is the one most frequently used with the voice of the operator. Good glove puppetry tends to be strong, comic, with plenty of action using props. If you are planning to make a show for yourself to perform, it is also the type of puppet most easily used in a solo show, because you can have two puppets performing at a time.

Rod puppetry

The next puppet for increasing your vocabulary is from the largest group of puppet types. Rod puppets can be very small or very, very tall (see Figs. 13–17, 50, 51, 55, 56). They can be adapted in many ways to fit the needs of anyone; they can be very light and made comfortable for holding. Special attention might have to be given to adjusting hand grips and controls (see Fig. 17 and plate 12). In some cases whole puppets might have to be designed with a particular client in mind. For people confined to wheelchairs, it may be necessary to have specially designed puppets.

Wheelchairs provide marvellous scope for gadgetry. Once, a group of my students found in their research that those who were quite alert but very physically challenged enjoyed puppets designed to do amusing but simple things such as drinking out of a bottle or having a fight. The students produced gadgets, with no end of possibilities, ranging from some very simple rod puppets attached to the arm rest to elaborate Heath Robinson affairs with weights and pulleys.

Rod puppets are better at gesture than glove puppets because their limbs can be longer and more expressive.

Simple Rod Puppets

Fig. 13.

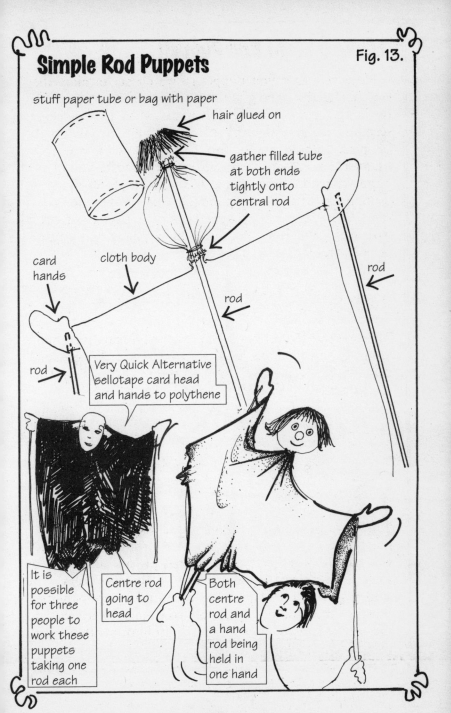

stuff paper tube or bag with paper

hair glued on

gather filled tube at both ends tightly onto central rod

card hands

cloth body

rod

rod

rod

Very Quick Alternative sellotape card head and hands to polythene

It is possible for three people to work these puppets taking one rod each

Centre rod going to head

Both centre rod and a hand rod being held in one hand

25

Make a Giant Rod Puppet!

Fig. 14.

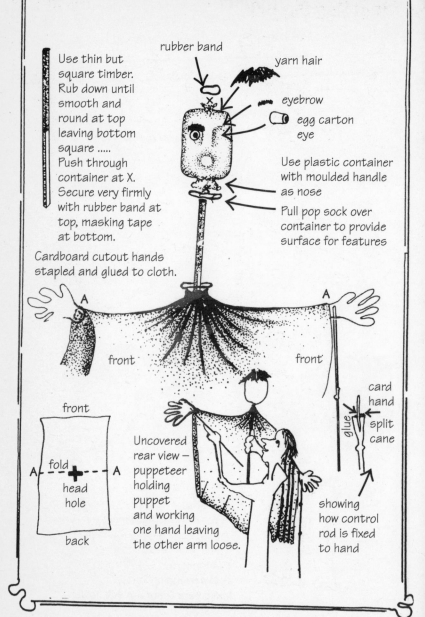

Use thin but square timber. Rub down until smooth and round at top leaving bottom square .....
Push through container at X. Secure very firmly with rubber band at top, masking tape at bottom.

rubber band

yarn hair

eyebrow

egg carton eye

Use plastic container with moulded handle as nose

Pull pop sock over container to provide surface for features

Cardboard cutout hands stapled and glued to cloth.

A

front

front

A

card hand

glue

split cane

front

fold

A

A

head hole

back

Uncovered rear view — puppeteer holding puppet and working one hand leaving the other arm loose.

showing how control rod is fixed to hand

See also photograph – plate 1.

26

Giant Rod Puppet ...

Fig. 15.

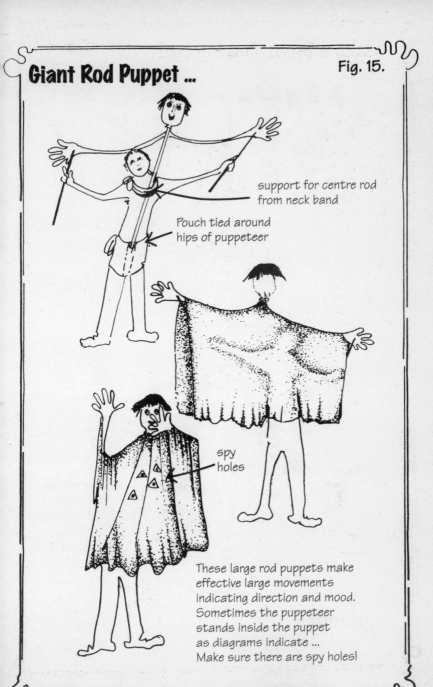

support for centre rod from neck band

Pouch tied around hips of puppeteer

spy holes

These large rod puppets make effective large movements indicating direction and mood. Sometimes the puppeteer stands inside the puppet as diagrams indicate ... Make sure there are spy holes!

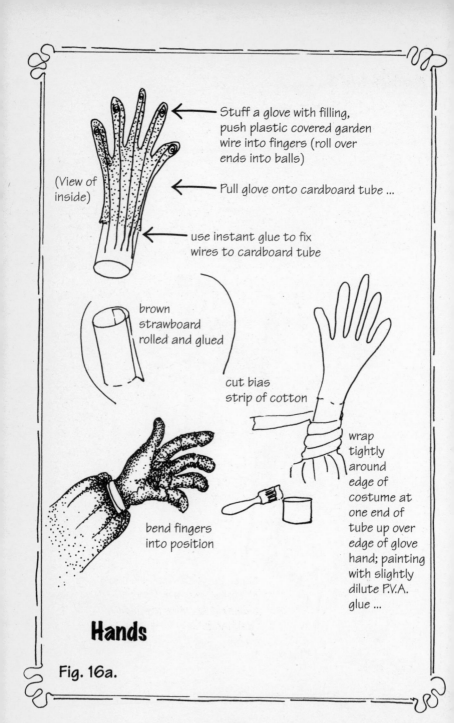

Stuff a glove with filling, push plastic covered garden wire into fingers (roll over ends into balls)

(View of inside)

Pull glove onto cardboard tube ...

use instant glue to fix wires to cardboard tube

brown strawboard rolled and glued

cut bias strip of cotton

wrap tightly around edge of costume at one end of tube up over edge of glove hand; painting with slightly dilute P.V.A. glue ...

bend fingers into position

Hands

Fig. 16a.

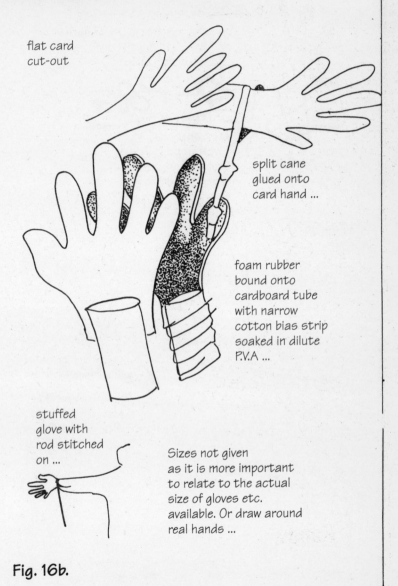

flat card
cut-out

split cane
glued onto
card hand ...

foam rubber
bound onto
cardboard tube
with narrow
cotton bias strip
soaked in dilute
P.V.A ...

stuffed
glove with
rod stitched
on ...

Sizes not given
as it is more important
to relate to the actual
size of gloves etc.
available. Or draw around
real hands ...

Fig. 16b.

Feet

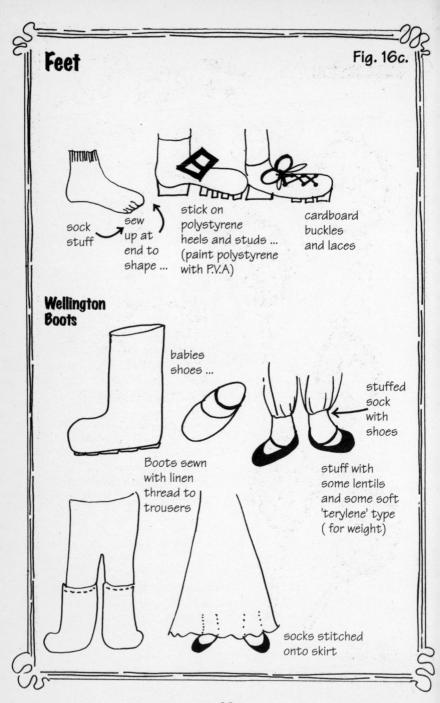

sock
stuff

sew
up at
end to
shape ...

stick on
polystyrene
heels and studs ...
(paint polystyrene
with P.V.A)

cardboard
buckles
and laces

Wellington Boots

babies
shoes ...

stuffed
sock
with
shoes

Boots sewn
with linen
thread to
trousers

stuff with
some lentils
and some soft
'terylene' type
(for weight)

socks stitched
onto skirt

30

Expression

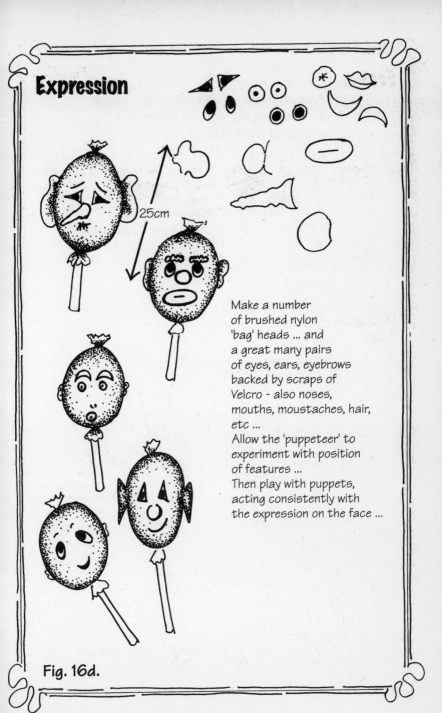

25cm

Make a number
of brushed nylon
'bag' heads ... and
a great many pairs
of eyes, ears, eyebrows
backed by scraps of
Velcro - also noses,
mouths, moustaches, hair,
etc ...
Allow the 'puppeteer' to
experiment with position
of features ...
Then play with puppets,
acting consistently with
the expression on the face ...

Fig. 16d.

Noses

Puppets need strong prominent noses
so that you can control where your
puppet is looking ...

x section

block of polystyrene –
cut out shaded area ...
push into nose two
pieces of stiff wire.
Use the wire to push into
the polystyrene head ...

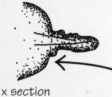

x section

← paint surface with slightly
dilute P.V.A.

stocking head

twist

tie off
tightly

cork

egg-box
piece ...

foam rubber

chip off foam
piece by piece
by snipping with
scissors or picking
off with fingers

or roll up
flat piece
of foam

sew tightly
at intervals
to give shape ...

Fig. 16e.

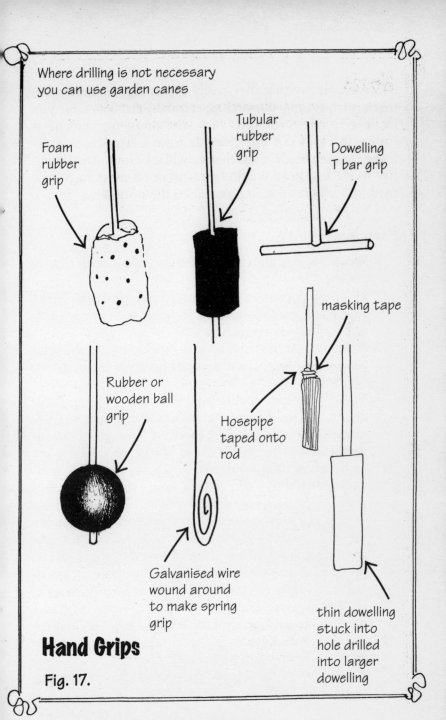

Where drilling is not necessary you can use garden canes

Foam rubber grip

Tubular rubber grip

Dowelling T bar grip

masking tape

Rubber or wooden ball grip

Hosepipe taped onto rod

Galvanised wire wound around to make spring grip

thin dowelling stuck into hole drilled into larger dowelling

Hand Grips

Fig. 17.

Some people say that they easily depict supernatural creatures, such as angels, witches, wizards, etc. I suggest you
make a simple traditional one—the one I recommend is
shown in Fig. 13. It can be made from a large black polythene rubbish bag, or, alternatively black cloth. An alternative to the bag head would be to cut out a mask face from
card and sellotape it straight on to the polythene.

Exercises

1 Work in pairs with one person watching, then change
   places.
2 Hold the puppet up and away from your body. Make
   sure you are standing well and ready with knees loose,
   not locked into your hips.
3 Hold both of the hand rods in one hand, and the head
   rod in the other. (Leaving rods hanging can cause an
   accident).
4 Move your own hands around without letting go of
   the rods. Don't wave but rather move into one position with one move, then stop. You might find it
   useful to look in the mirror as you do this. Find some
   really interesting positions.
5 Your partner should put up a finger and slowly move
   it around, changing direction when he or she feels
   like it. The person operating the puppet should make
   the eyes of the puppet follow your partner's finger
   very closely—this will show the 'intelligence' of the
   puppet—if the eyes of the puppet cannot fix on to
   anything, then the puppet will never be effective.
6 Make sure you keep the puppet in front of you—
   don't try to look around the front at what the puppet
   is doing. You have to get used to watching from the
   back (sorry to spoil your fun!)
7 As a group, hold your puppets up and each take one
   of the following words or phrases:

Old
King-Cole
Was a
Merry
Old
Soul
and a
Merry
Old
Soul
Was he.

8 Make a frozen position for your word. For example, for '*Old*' you might bend the puppet forward to look hunched, and put both hands together, as if they were resting on a stick. '*King Cole*' might be both hands up high on either side of the puppet's head to indicate a crown. '*Was a*' could be both arms to the front to include everyone—more of a shrug, and so on. When you have chosen your movement, then put the whole phrase together, one person after another, all standing in a circle making their movement. Keep on going around the circle—you will find that you will have to learn other moves—until you can repeat the phrase fluently. Great fun—in case you had your doubts.

9 Another exercise is to choose a simple country dance with music, and teach it to each other, and dance away. Keep the puppets very close together—it is what they are doing, not what you are doing, that matters.

10 Make sure you put your arms down and rest frequently.

11 Finally, go back to your fairy tale. Retell it now, using the tableau technique (see the glove puppetry exercises on p. 19) but mixing rod puppets with glove puppets. Choose the roles according to the story and what the puppet has to offer in terms of what it can do and

what the story needs. Use a narrator. There is no need for the puppets to speak at this stage.

12 You will find that all this activity with the puppets is going to make you move more and more, so restrict any movement of the puppets to gesturing on the spot.

There is another very popular type of rod puppet, and this is called the table-top puppet because that is where it is usually operated with the puppeteer in full view (see Fig. 18. This was designed for a 'healthy eating project.' Fig. 11 is also a table-top puppet but a glove-type. See also plates 10 & 19).

Chef Puppet

Fig. 18.

An easily manipulated puppet combining the size and strong head movement of a rod puppet and the ease of handling props of a glove puppet.

bag head on rod held in one hand can nod and shake ...

false hand attached to costume

Puppeteer's own hand to hold plate with photograph of food – The group can choose other pictures of food to "serve"

Shadow puppetry

This is a marvellous medium. It seems to work for all ages and types of person. It can be very large scale and very small scale. (See plates 2 & 3, 11 & 14). There are some examples of puppet types to make (see Figs 19–24) and exercises to go with them. For the light source I would recommend an overhead projector for all your early work. It is a safe and versatile piece of equipment. An ordinary box type one is best—better than the flat executive type. In the latter, images become doubled whereas it is easy to blend in the former type.

In addition to making puppets, you also need to make a colour wheel (see Fig. 25b). For this you simply need a piece of clear Perspex—thin enough to cut into a large circle; sellotape pieces of lighting colours Cinemoid or Lee on to this or use coloured cellophane. Although I have included instructions for making simple shadow screens (see Figs 31 and 33), you will also need to make a large screen. I use soft polyester lining fabric sewn together to make a large screen 3 widths by about 5 metres. I usually tape it to long canes and the group takes turns holding it up, or else I tape the canes to the legs of two chairs with masking tape (see Fig. 25a).

Traditionally, puppet-makers explored different ways to allow light to pass through the puppet. The Javanese Fig. 19a, puppet-maker plays with contrast of light against dark by punching a design through the body of the puppet (see Fig. 19a). The Turkish shadow puppet is made from a thin skin, dyed in a variety of colours and then oiled to make it transparent. Long slashes are cut to let through extra light (see Fig. 19b).

Fig. 19a.

Note exaggerated size of shoulders – the important aspect of this puppet

Whole puppet is rigid apart from arms ... (no emphasis on the mouth as part of a functional head) The expressiveness of the puppet rests in the arms ...

joints (overlap)

Highly decorated, stylised human form.

rod

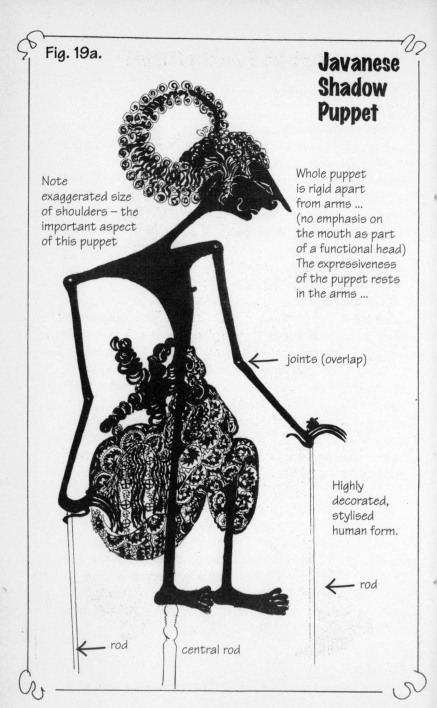

rod

central rod

Turkish Shadow Puppet

(More figurative
than the Javanese
type)

control hole

Note the size
of head and
therefore the
importance of
speech.

In designing
puppets for your
own use emphasise
the parts of the
puppet which
demonstrate an
important aspect
of the character.

control
hole for
horizontal
rods.

more joints ∴
more vigorous
movement

Fig. 19b.

Fig. 19c.

wire stuck with strong glue into bamboo-cane

horizontal rod ... sewn onto puppet to make a hinged control

Use carpet thread to knot cat legs on the sides of body as shown —

All these shadow puppets need horizontal rods ...

card cut-out cheese on rod ...

Fig. 20.

Cat

A Shadow Puppet ... with props ...

Fig. 21.

Props may be simply taped to the hand ...

arms should be free to move ... Use a spare rod to knock the arms up and down ...

rod

Attach cane to body on reverse side to arms ...

glue bamboo cane all along length to keep puppet rigid ...

Paint over rod with black paint ... Turn rod in the hand to go in one direction or another

Every prop needs a rod

Foam rubber. If your grip is weak

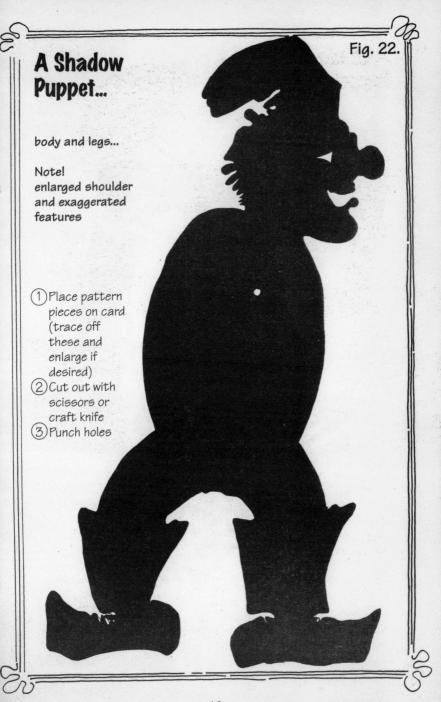

A Shadow Puppet...

body and legs...

Note!
enlarged shoulder
and exaggerated
features

① Place pattern
pieces on card
(trace off
these and
enlarge if
desired)
② Cut out with
scissors or
craft knife
③ Punch holes

Fig. 22.

43

Shadow Puppet

arm pattern...

Note!
exaggerated features

④ Put arms across body, matching
holes, fix with paper fastener — make
sure arms can move freely...

Fig. 23.

Use craft knife to cut
stripes on tiger.
If necessary strengthen
with clear sellotape ...

jointed jaw

Legs swing freely

Put together as
for cat.
Using horizontal rods.

Fig. 24.

45

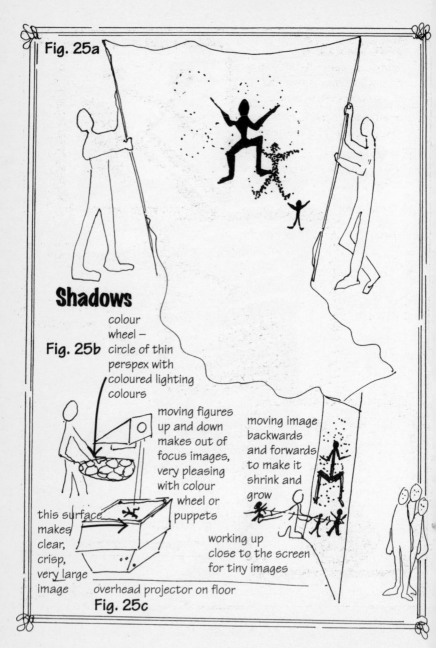

Fig. 25a

Shadows

Fig. 25b colour
wheel —
circle of thin
perspex with
coloured lighting
colours

moving figures
up and down
makes out of
focus images,
very pleasing
with colour
wheel or
puppets

moving image
backwards
and forwards
to make it
shrink and
grow

this surface
makes
clear,
crisp,
very large
image

working up
close to the screen
for tiny images

overhead projector on floor

Fig. 25c

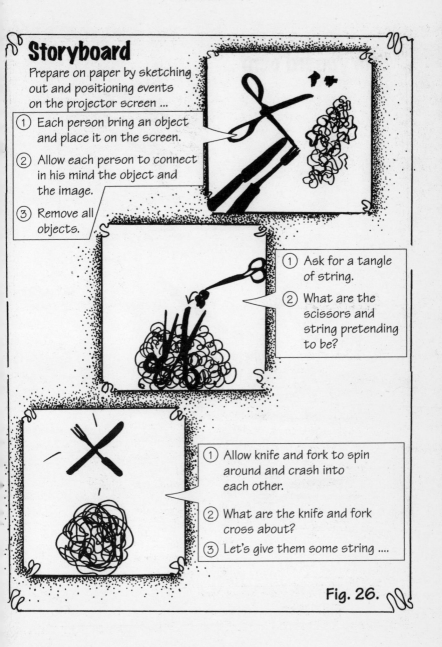

Storyboard

Prepare on paper by sketching
out and positioning events
on the projector screen ...

① Each person bring an object
and place it on the screen.

② Allow each person to connect
in his mind the object and
the image.

③ Remove all
objects.

① Ask for a tangle
of string.

② What are the
scissors and
string pretending
to be?

① Allow knife and fork to spin
around and crash into
each other.

② What are the knife and fork
cross about?

③ Let's give them some string ....

Fig. 26.

Storyboard cont ...

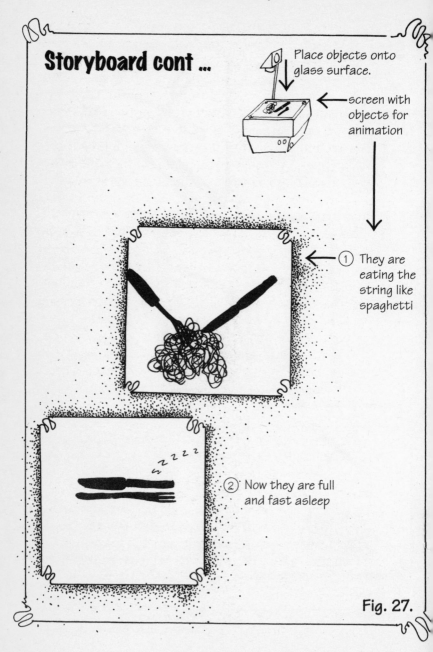

Place objects onto glass surface.

screen with objects for animation

① They are eating the string like spaghetti

② Now they are full and fast asleep

Fig. 27.

Section 1

Exercises

There are three useful areas to play on when using the overhead projector (See Fig. 25a).

1 The flat glass—if you place your puppet on that it projects very large and clear.
2 The second playing area is between the mirror and the flat glass. If you lift your figure up, it will go out of focus and get bigger. Put the figure back on to the flat glass and slide the colour wheel into the playing area. Turn it around using both hands, but make sure you keep them out of the light. You will find that you are able to change the mood for the puppet on the flat glass, by moving the different colours into view.
3 The third playing area on the overhead projector is the area between the overhead projector and the screen. Attach the puppet to a rod with some masking-tape—turn it flat, facing the screen and move it closer slowly. You will see that it is large and out of focus, which is fine—but the closer it comes to the screen the more in focus it becomes, until it is clean and small as it touches the screen.
4 Take a fish puppet and put it on to the screen where it will look small. Put another fish puppet with a great big open mouth on to the flat glass. Change the colour wheel to blue. Make the little front screen fish swim into the mouth of the big fish.
5 This exercise will put together all three elements. Using the big soft screen, any puppets and the colour wheel, two people hold the canes supporting the screen and waft the screen backwards and forwards. Keep changing the puppets on the flat glass screen and keep the colour wheel moving slowly. Play with the wafting of the cloth—some spectators might like to go underneath the cloth as well as watching from

49

the front—the mix of colours can be made even more exciting if you have two wheels working at the same time.
6 Try the ideas from Figs 26–27.

Marionettes

> 'The line which the centre of gravity must describe was something very mysterious, for it was no less than the path of the dancer's soul, and he doubted that it could be found except by the puppeteer transposing himself into the centre of gravity of the marionette: in other words, by dancing' Heinrich von Kleist (tr. Christopher Halsall) for Animations.

The marionette is often of interest to boys—possibly it is the technical aspects of string puppets that are so attractive to them. Your own puppet-operating practice requires one of these magnificent puppets. The discipline of operating one improves all your puppetry (and to be watched playing with one definitely impresses your friends). Our home from time to time is bursting with puppeteers carving in our cellar-workshop. Gradually after four or five days the puppets are completed, strung, and then for the first time walked—most students say it is like a birth. (See plate 20).

Well, here we are not looking at the carved wooden figure for client use, because that is probably something for your future, but two very simple workshop types that are suspended by strings (based on the traditional Rajasthani marioinette from India, see Fig. 28a), and another simple puppet suspended by a rod (based on the traditional folk rod marionettes, see Fig. 29a). Look at the instructions (Figs 28 and 29) and you should be able to make both of

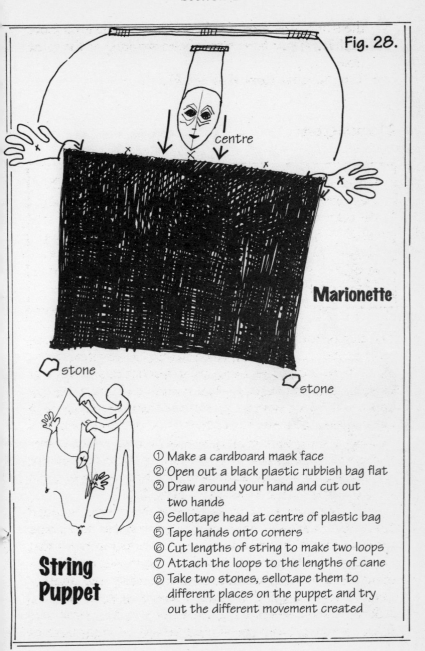

Fig. 28.

centre

Marionette

stone

stone

String Puppet

① Make a cardboard mask face
② Open out a black plastic rubbish bag flat
③ Draw around your hand and cut out two hands
④ Sellotape head at centre of plastic bag
⑤ Tape hands onto corners
⑥ Cut lengths of string to make two loops
⑦ Attach the loops to the lengths of cane
⑧ Take two stones, sellotape them to different places on the puppet and try out the different movement created

51

A Rajasthani Marionette

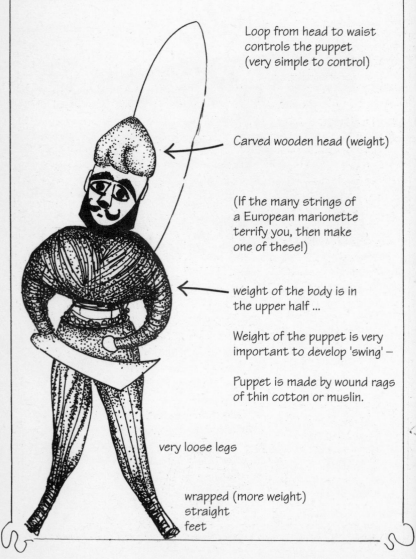

Loop from head to waist
controls the puppet
(very simple to control)

Carved wooden head (weight)

(If the many strings of
a European marionette
terrify you, then make
one of these!)

weight of the body is in
the upper half ...

Weight of the puppet is very
important to develop 'swing' –

Puppet is made by wound rags
of thin cotton or muslin.

very loose legs

wrapped (more weight)
straight
feet

Fig. 29.

Rod Marionette

① Make a hole in the bottom of a plastic bottle
② Push a cane or length of dowling through
③ Masking tape around the neck and the cane sticking out of the bottom to make it tight
④ Cut 4 slits 1, 2, 3, 4
⑤ Thread through two coloured plastic bags (thin plastic)
⑥ Tie knots to make hands and feet

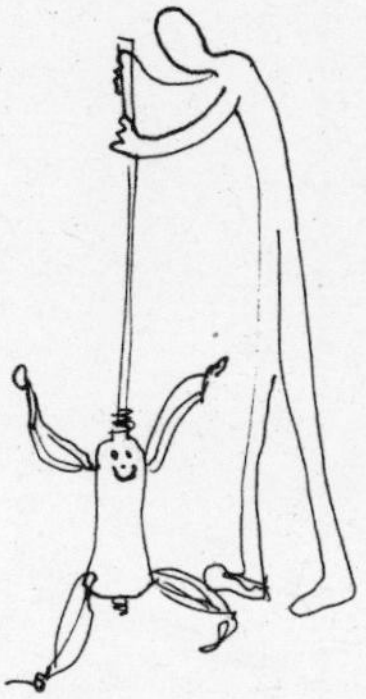

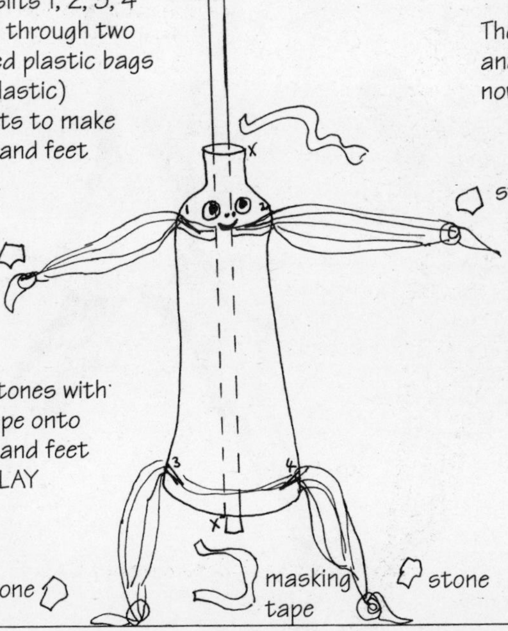

⑦ Tape stones with sellotape onto hands and feet AND PLAY

Swing the puppet by twisting the rod from side to side and lifting up and down

The arms and legs will now swing

stone

stone

stone

stone

masking tape

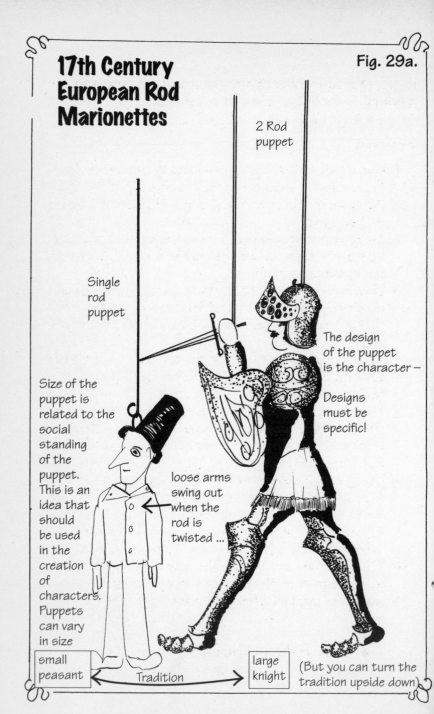

17th Century European Rod Marionettes

2 Rod puppet

Single rod puppet

The design of the puppet is the character —

Designs must be specific!

Size of the puppet is related to the social standing of the puppet. This is an idea that should be used in the creation of characters. Puppets can vary in size

loose arms swing out when the rod is twisted ...

small peasant

large knight

Tradition

(But you can turn the tradition upside down)

them. One attraction of the marionette is that you are working a whole figure which usually has legs.

Exercises

1 Use a piece of string approximately one metre long. Let it dangle down on to the ground. Let it fly above the ground or drag on the ground. How much control do you have?

2 Tie a weight of some kind on to the end of the string. Play again with the weight. Swing it, drag it, vary all the possible types of movement.

3 Now have a movement 'dialogue' with another weight on string—two people working together. Keep going without talking—see what ranges of movement you achieve together.

4 Tie another piece of string on to the weight. What does that do to your control of the object?

5 Make another movement 'dialogue'.

6 Note that you are using gravity, the ground and strings to give you control. Swing it to give movement.

7 Now use the basic string puppet you have made (Fig. 28). Fly it around.

8 Using stones and sellotape, try putting a stone into each corner of the hem of the puppet—what effect does this have on the puppet's movement?

9 Remove these stones and put a stone in each elbow. What effect does that have on the movement?

10 When you are happy with the way the puppet moves, walk the puppet, fly it, make it crawl, jump, turn, etc.

11 Move the puppet across space for ten counts. Turn it to:

- stare at the audience
- react to the audience.

Turn and go away for ten counts.
12 Using the rod marionette (Fig. 29), play the game of sticky toffee. One puppet is 'it'. Chase the puppets until one puppet is caught. The puppets join hands and the two of them, without letting go of each other, give chase to the others, until the hands of all the puppets are joined. You have to make sure that you are only making puppet-sized steps and not dragging the puppets around while you yourself are taking chase. *Remember you are working through the puppets not using the puppets as a weapon.*

Stages, booths and tables

As a puppeteer, I often have to build stages designed for a particular job. But if you go to the trouble of getting something built too early on, you might find that you have a white elephant on your hands. It is much better to improvise for as long as possible until you have had some experience. However, below, I shall give you some guidelines.

Try working at a table (see Figs 30 and 31)
A table provides a useful barrier between you, any spectators and the group. It is somewhere to rest your arms—and makes you use the whole arm for glove puppetry and not just the wrist and hand. It gives a special dimension to your work—underneath, on top, behind, in front. This might be important for language work. The table provides formality. It is known as a place where one eats, works, plays some games. It is a place of activity. It is best for table-top rod and glove puppetry but Fig. 31 is a shadow screen clamped on to the top of a table.

Encourage members of the group to keep a good sitting position. Ask them to stand up and sit down a few times—

Where to Work... open exercises...

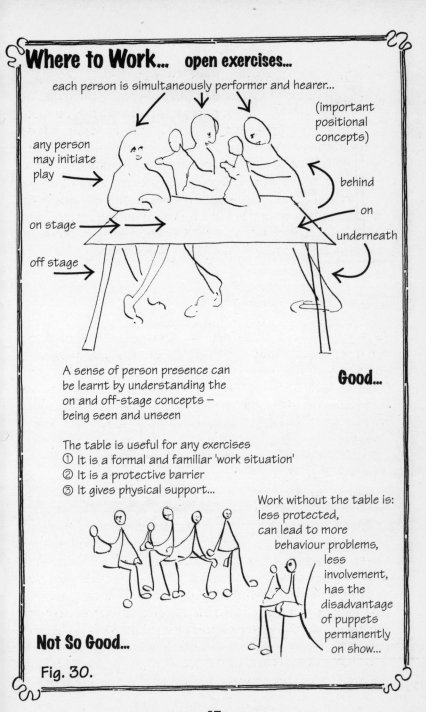

each person is simultaneously performer and hearer...

(important positional concepts)

any person may initiate play →

behind

on

on stage →

underneath

off stage →

A sense of person presence can be learnt by understanding the on and off-stage concepts — being seen and unseen

Good...

The table is useful for any exercises
① It is a formal and familiar 'work situation'
② It is a protective barrier
③ It gives physical support...

Work without the table is: less protected, can lead to more behaviour problems, less involvement, has the disadvantage of puppets permanently on show...

Not So Good...

Fig. 30.

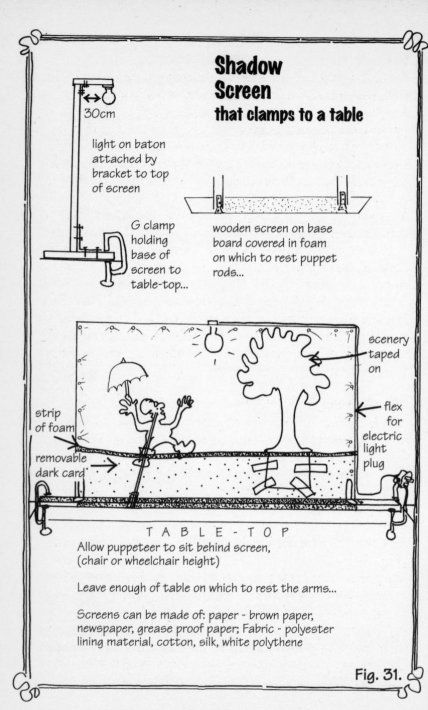

Shadow Screen
that clamps to a table

30cm

light on baton
attached by
bracket to top
of screen

G clamp
holding
base of
screen to
table-top...

wooden screen on base
board covered in foam
on which to rest puppet
rods...

scenery
taped
on

flex
for
electric
light
plug

strip
of foam

removable
dark card

TABLE-TOP

Allow puppeteer to sit behind screen,
(chair or wheelchair height)

Leave enough of table on which to rest the arms...

Screens can be made of: paper - brown paper,
newspaper, grease proof paper; Fabric - polyester
lining material, cotton, silk, white polythene

Fig. 31.

58

make it a game. Always check on their sitting and standing balance. Do this with anyone, but it is most appropriate for those with learning or physical disabilities. Take turns passing the puppets around—try to pass them from person to person, keeping them alive as you go. Hot-seat one of the characters—the whole group takes turns asking the puppet questions to find out likes and dislikes.

You should aim to establish the table-top as the playing area, stage or playboard. Make a great deal of this. Stick coloured paper down on to the surface to emphasis the playing area. Think of this part of your work as the introduction of performance skills rather than random play. What happened during the improvisation? Did you allow anyone to lie across the table, put their heads down or go to sleep? This special place should become identified with the use of the puppets, then you will find fewer attempts to sprawl on it.

Try the tipped-up table booth (Fig. 32)
If your group can stand and move about easily, then this is fine as a temporary arrangement. Only one or two people can work at a time, but you can encourage a continuous flow of spectators to help with the decision-making. An enclosed booth-like space encourages hiding—so not so highly recommended.

Try the loo tent with a hole cut out at the front (Fig. 34)
Why this has caused to much hilarity whenever I have mentioned it in a lecture, I am not sure. When I started as a puppeteer as the first UK Punch and Judy Lady, I did my research and looked at pictures of the Punch men and their booths—which looked to me like tents. So I went to the tent shop in Harrogate—and chose the one which was ready erected, bright blue and exactly the right size and

Where to Work... concealed exercises...

Each person has to <u>make a choice</u> to move behind the table. The table is not big enough to take everyone so there is a continuous flow between performing watching performing — Number of puppets in use at one time is limited...

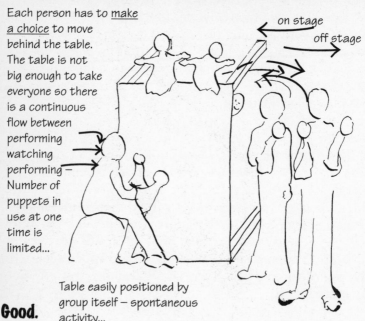

on stage

off stage

Good.

Table easily positioned by group itself — spontaneous activity...

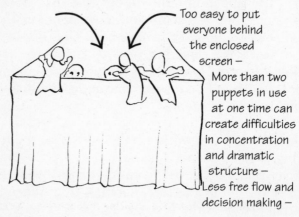

Too easy to put everyone behind the enclosed screen —
More than two puppets in use at one time can create difficulties in concentration and dramatic structure —
Less free flow and decision making —

Not So Good.

Also — <u>your</u> students are not visible!

Fig. 32.

Where to Work... the shadow screen...

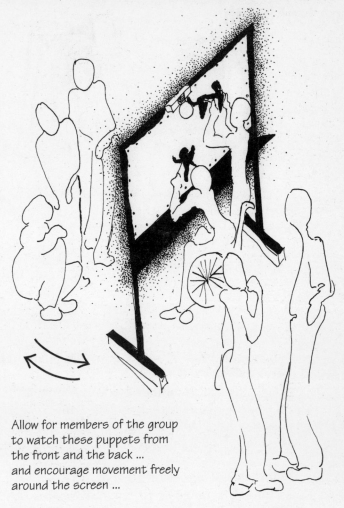

Allow for members of the group
to watch these puppets from
the front and the back ...
and encourage movement freely
around the screen ...

The screen is to become an exciting and special place
in the same way as the table-booth and the table-top ...

Fig. 33.

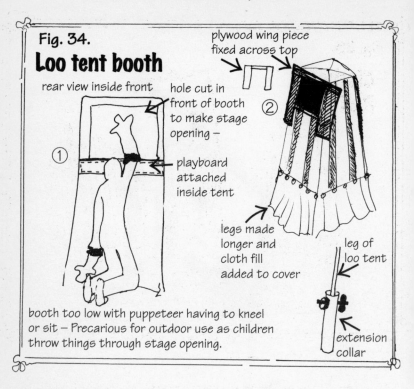

Fig. 34.

Loo tent booth

rear view inside front

plywood wing piece fixed across top

hole cut in front of booth to make stage opening –

②

①

playboard attached inside tent

legs made longer and cloth fill added to cover

leg of loo tent

extension collar

booth too low with puppeteer having to kneel or sit – Precarious for outdoor use as children throw things through stage opening.

shape. I bought it and took it home, read the guarantee and found it was called a toilet tent. Not being a camper, I hadn't realised. Nor did it bother me. I recommend it, but you do need to make it higher if you want to work standing up—which I did. In class, though, I do not think anything that is closed in all the way round is a good idea.

Try the old clothes rail—best of all (Fig. 35)
Clothes rails come in a range of prices and weights. The cheapest might push over. Using canes and tape you can adapt the height from a sitting position to standing, you can also link several up to make a variety of shapes and levels and it is useful for every type of puppet (shadow, glove, rod) except the marionette. (See also Fig. 33).

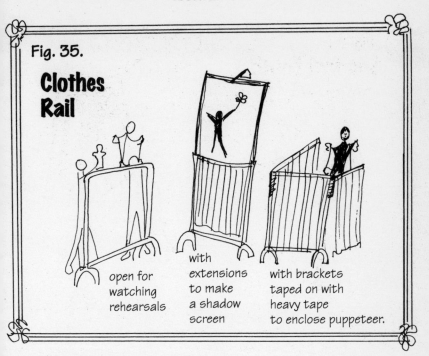

Fig. 35.

Clothes Rail

open for watching rehearsals

with extensions to make a shadow screen

with brackets taped on with heavy tape to enclose puppeteer.

You should now have a selection of simply and quickly made puppets. From now on all your work should be operating and playing with them. In schools very precious objects are made from papier mâché, cloth, even clay—some teachers even assure me that they will, at some future date, make a puppet show—but then term ends and the objects are taken home and that, as they say, is that. *Those objects never become puppets.* But to finish this section on a positive note—let us not call your puppets precious objects, but rather the tools for the job—and it is the job you do with them that will be precious.

Section 2

Puppet theatre
The uniqueness of puppetry
Some history of puppet theatre/parody/
    therapy: notable features
Character building
Storybuilding
Music
Collaborations

Puppet theatre

> 'Like a fish out of water, the puppet out of performance is a dead thing, a potential signifier only.' Roman Paska

I started off in youth theatre, so I was used to every aspect of the work, especially performing, by the time I discovered puppetry in my late twenties. Learning to perform with the puppet was a matter of picking it up and putting it in front of you and then acting along with it. And even though I was performing with puppets for a while I don't think I started *learning* and growing as a performer until I started to teach, and then it was more or less based on what was boring and what was not, and whether I could see what was being shown to me, and whether we were all enjoying ourselves. Theatre director, Wilfred Harrison, invited me to play in Bolton for the Octagon Theatre and took me out to lunch after I had finished my performance: 'Wonderful energy my dear, but too much of it, you need directing,' he commented.

I thought it was *necessary* for the puppeteer to move around and do things at the same time as the puppet. I was quite proud of my bright red face and the sweat pouring off me after a performance, as it showed everyone how hard I was working.

Realising my need to learn properly, with an Arts Council Bursary, I went to London and started a period of a few months at the Little Angel Marionette Theatre. At first I had to learn by sitting quietly watching the puppeteers operating their marionettes for the public shows. They hardly moved their own bodies at all. Wonderful energy was being channelled right into the puppets. The puppeteers had stored the memory of every movement in their imaginations, ready to send it down the strings to be realised in the carved wooden figure at the other end: more dance than drama.

Later on, when working with choreographer Wendy Cook, we researched this sense of movement, calling it kinaesthetics. Movement starts in the body of the puppeteer from a previous time; it then resides in the memory of the puppeteer before being realised once again in the puppet. It is the lack of movement sense that causes someone to waggle and shake their puppets.

The uniqueness of puppetry

My first training after leaving school was to stage-manage opera. Opera singers never used to move very much. The orchestral players did and were more interesting to draw. I had so many free tickets to sit in royal boxes that I would use the time drawing musicians. Opera singers tended not to move off the spot. During my year studying puppetry, care of the Arts Council, I went to a Ballet Rambert season at the old Sadlers Wells. I realised that I had forgotten about movement on stage and now I feasted. I also had to rethink my ideas about puppetry because, apart from marionettes, puppets did not leave base, because they nearly always had the puppeteer attached to them like an anchor. Everything about a puppet is its movement, but pared down and selected: a representation of human, animal or object movement—not an exaggeration of it.

Puppet theatre is unique and it is a hybrid. Essentially a visual art, it calls on whatever is necessary to make a performance, but it is not drama, nor is it dance, nor is it moving pictures, nor moving sculptures—but it *is* a visual performing art with its own disciplines and traditions that might draw on those other art forms—usually to parody them. In fact I would say that parody is the major way of making puppet theatre.

Some history of puppet theatre parody therapy: notable features

Puppet theatre is an ancient and popular entertainment. In Ancient Greece when the cities could no longer afford the great plays of Euripides, it was the marionettist Potheinos who entertained the crowds or took performances into the streets for people to see. Although they were often secretly delighted by it, in public great personages despised puppet theatre because it belonged to ordinary poor people. It was also subversive and set itself up to question and ridicule the *status quo*. There was a tradition in Western society to regard popular culture as low, because it was (and is) accessible to the man in the street and the marketplace.

'To Southworke Fair, very dirty, and there saw the Puppet-show of Whittington, which was pretty to see; and how that idle thing doth work upon people that see it, *and even myself too*.' Samuel Pepys, *Diary*, 21 September 1668

And what about the street? The street levels out all classes because everyone is there and has a right to be so. Few puppeteers have celebrated the despised roots of puppetry more than Bread and Puppet Theatre in the USA with their immense processions in the Sixties, in which they parodied the culture of the Bomb and US imperialism. Horse and Bamboo took to the streets in a horse-drawn cart to take shows all over the UK and Europe. Richard Robinson with his Oggle Oggle Box performed throughout the 1980s, satirising Margaret Thatcher—he created clones of her and her Cabinet through their efforts to influence Flo Tingvoter.

Before puppetry was a therapeutic resource it was theatre, albeit popular and rooted wherever the populace gathered. No one knew how it worked but, as the saying goes, they knew what they liked. Puppetry appeared to empower the spectator, it addressed their concerns, it satirised their overlords and did to them what they would love to do themselves, in fact it parodied the culture they lived in and showed up hypocrisy.

It was Sigmund Freud who looked at theatre and our relationship to it—and later on it was D. W. Winnicott who explored the use of objects in childhood play and who coined the phrase 'transitional object'. But can we benefit our clients by involving them in the disciplines of theatre. Let us look at what puppet theatre has to offer:

Our guiding principle is the impulse in every human being to respond to objects as if they are alive (whether by operating them themselves or by participating as a spectator).

Section 2

- *Puppetry is inherently humorous*—although it is not necessary for parody to be funny, often it is the odd juxtaposition of images or ideas that causes mirth. Even in the therapeutic sphere, a discussion between an abused child and a toy hedgehog takes place— even in that tragic context it is humour opening the door to healing.
- *In puppet theatre there is robust play between* any *objects replacing vulnerable human interaction.*
- *Puppet theatre can show an event at an objective distance and by using drama overturn the* status quo. The strong are overcome by the weak. Social norms and rules of etiquette are upturned; politicians are satirised; Miss Piggy interviews the wives of US presidents; Emu brings down the mighty Michael Parkinson. Puppetry parodies high and elitist culture. It tests boundaries of decency. The puppets of *Spitting Image* inveigled their way on to our screens to celebrate the viewer over men and women of power who think they hold our strings.
- *Puppet theatre is celebratory.* We can enjoy and celebrate this essential aspect of humanness in puppet-play. We can take the time to mark out periods of our lives as specific, for note, as in this age of agnosticism, the loss of ancient festivals is a loss to our lives lived in the social sphere. Advanced age, unemployment, disablement, steal away the rhythm of work and relaxation and with them the point of seasonal celebration.

Puppet theatre has traditions and characteristics that are worth exploring practically. The roots of puppetry are from the streets and open places. They were places of danger and there will be times when you might work with people who are clearly in danger. Although there is scope for humour—a good street emotion—processions can be

71

What is Drama?
Choosing a hero

Fig. 36.

Punch – what kind of character is he? Bombastic, greedy, cheeky? He wants a kiss from his wife Judy – What is she like? houseproud... always busy so she does not take kindly to Punch's demands – These ideas which are certainly in opposition result in action!

What is Drama?

Fig. 37.

opposing ideas in action

Punch – (we know him by the way he looks, acts, moves, speaks) → meets Policeman (we know him by the way he looks acts, moves, speaks) → something happens. What?

The characters must be consistent with their make-up

Fig. 38.

Punch does not
take kindly to being
tickled but being the
bombastic creature he is –
he reacts violently with his
slapstick...

What are the
consequences of
this action...?
How may the
drama continue?

What is Drama?

moving and emotional—there is in the puppet a potential for sadness. Puppet theatre is, essentially, built out of the interaction of characters.

Character building

Choosing a hero
Our first exercise will be to explore the idea of an 'everyman' or 'everywoman'. In the history of puppet theatre there are some figures with whom it is easy to identify because they are supposedly just like us. They make mistakes, they get things wrong, they try hard and things work out in the end in some way or another. They are instantly appealing because they are so fallible. Famous names are Punch, Caspar, Kariogoz. It is important to find a hero of this type; otherwise you are left with the bad characters who are always being more interesting than the good ones (something I find unsatisfactory). When you are working with, for example, abused children—you need to have a very definite idea of right and wrong, good and bad. The 'everyman/everywoman' kind of character is appealing because s/he is not perfect.

This exercise is to create—first of all on paper—a hero character.

Exercise
1 Roll out a large piece of lining paper on to a long table or on to the floor.
2 Draw your hero—as simply and as roughly as you like.
3 Give him a special prop to hold.
4 Talk about what he or she is like (Fig. 36).
5 Talk about what he or she wants (Fig. 36).
6 Talk about what happens when two heroes meet (Figs 36–38).

75

Storybuilding

Looking at characters for dramatic potential

Look at the drawings of Punch to get an idea of what we mean by 'dramatic potential'. Characters need to be strongly contrasted for the story to flow along (see Figs 36–38).

Allow everyone in the group to imagine some characters, but, for the sake of illustration, I have drawn some examples and put in some character notes. A character is identified by the way s/he looks and the way s/he acts. Although *we* can also handle incongruity and surprises—sometimes someone with learning disabilities or an audience with special needs might need *extra reinforcement* of the character, using very clear movement and music. I used to give every puppet its own song as a way of distilling plot and character into a few easily repeated lines—great fun but you'd know I wasn't a musician. The emphasis here is on two characters meeting, but of course we know that dramatic contrast can come out of a single character having a struggle with an idea inside him or a prop—this might be called a monologue or a soliloquy or just a solo; or dramatic contrast between groups of characters in conflict.

Invent the characters for the story

1 *Your choice: let us say Birgit, a girl who is a wheelchair user.*
2 *The King.* Fat, greedy, aggressive, with big boots and a crown, grows gold flowers which he carries (see Fig. 39).
3 *Fag Ash Lil.* Costume made from patches. Fag in her mouth, sweeping brush her main prop (see Fig. 40).
4 *Gretel the girl*—very fluffy, pink and white, carries a

Character

Fig. 39.

King

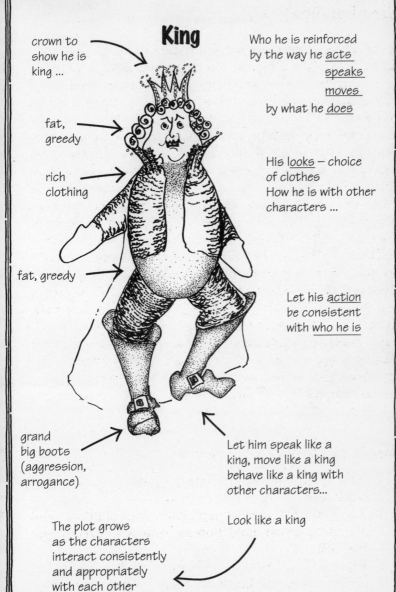

crown to
show he is
king ...

fat,
greedy

rich
clothing

fat, greedy

grand
big boots
(aggression,
arrogance)

Who he is reinforced
by the way he <u>acts</u>
                <u>speaks</u>
                <u>moves</u>
by what he <u>does</u>

His <u>looks</u> – choice
of clothes
How he is with other
characters ...

Let his <u>action</u>
be consistent
with <u>who he is</u>

Let him speak like a
king, move like a king
behave like a king with
other characters...

Look like a king

The plot grows
as the characters
interact consistently
and appropriately
with each other

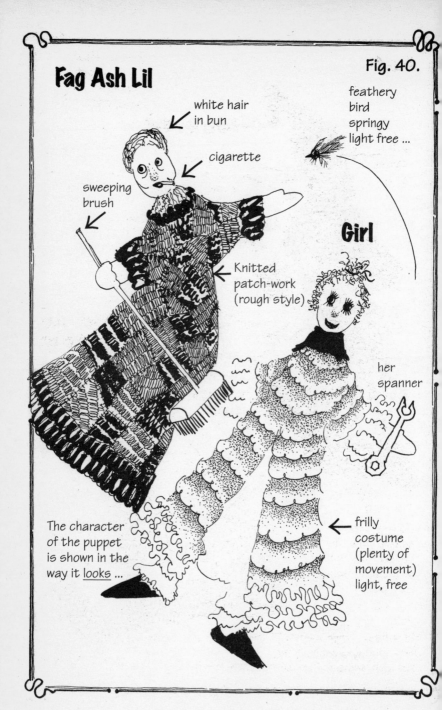

Fag Ash Lil

Fig. 40.

white hair in bun

cigarette

feathery bird springy light free ...

sweeping brush

Girl

Knitted patch-work (rough style)

her spanner

The character of the puppet is shown in the way it <u>looks</u> ...

frilly costume (plenty of movement) light, free

78

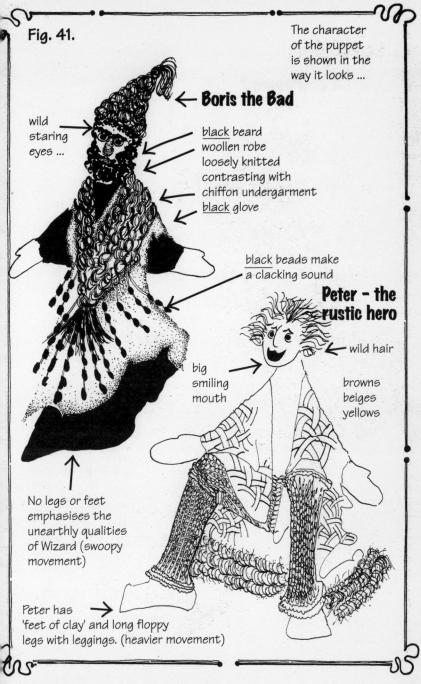

Fig. 41.

The character of the puppet is shown in the way it looks ...

← **Boris the Bad**

wild staring eyes ...

<u>black</u> beard
woollen robe
loosely knitted
contrasting with
chiffon undergarment
<u>black</u> glove

black beads make a clacking sound

Peter – the rustic hero

wild hair

big smiling mouth

browns
beiges
yellows

No legs or feet emphasises the unearthly qualities of Wizard (swoopy movement)

Peter has → 'feet of clay' and long floppy legs with leggings. (heavier movement)

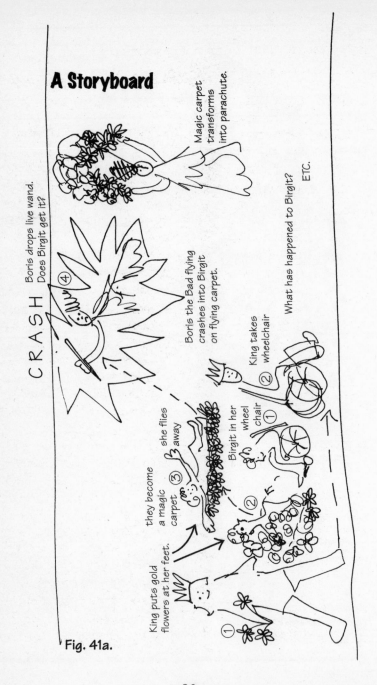

A Storyboard

Magic carpet transforms into parachute.

C R A S H   Boris drops live wand. Does Birgit get it?
④

Boris the Bad flying crashes into Birgit on flying carpet.

King takes wheelchair
②

What has happened to Birgit?

ETC.

they become a magic carpet   ③   she flies away

Birgit in her wheel chair
①

②

King puts gold flowers at her feet.

①

Fig. 41a.

80

Plate. 1
Rod puppets

Plate. 2
Shadow puppet
people playing
robots

Plate. 3
You can use
people to make
very large puppet
images

Plate. 4
Tubby

Plate. 5
Nicky's Humpty Dumpty

Plate. 6
Nicky's Mr Nosey and Whisky
the dog

Plate. 12 Visually challenged children rehearsing

Plate. 13
Giant 'people puppets' a two headed
giant operated by two people inside it

Plate. 14
Shadow puppet with human
character

Plate. 15 Word game with Hilary the Witch

Plate. 16 The child holds the puppet in one hand and uses her free hand for the activity to improve posture and complete the task

Plate. 17
Grandmother rod
puppet from
'Toothache'

Plate. 18
Meena Naik using
smaller puppets
for secret work
with young street
workers in
Bombay

Plate. 19
London School of
Puppetry students
using a variety of
table top puppets

Plate. 20
A Marionette
carved by a
London School of
Puppetry student

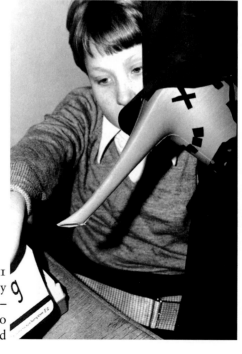

Plate. 21
Using Hilary
the Witch –
teaching her to
read

spanner because she's a plumber. She could also be a heroine (see Fig. 40).

5 *Little Feathery Bird* (see Fig. 40).

6 *Boris the Bad.* No legs, so that he's more magical. Beads that rattle on his costume. Carries a magic wand (see Fig. 41).

7 *Peter the Hero*, big floppy legs and wild hair. His main prop is his horse (see Fig. 41).

8 Still working on the lining paper, draw out the characters anywhere you like.

9 Now take them travelling—draw a dotted line to wherever they are going, and then redraw them where they encounter another character and have to stop (see Fig. 41a). Several stories will be happening simultaneously. Fig. 41a shows a fragment of a storyboard.

10 Something takes place when two characters meet—they have some kind of encounter and the consequences result from whatever contrasting qualities the characters have (Figs 36–38).

11 The rule of the game is that they can either exchange props or the prop is transformed into another totally different one.

This makes an exciting, often very amusing game. As the teacher, I found this fun to join in with—it helped me develop *my* ideas. In fact, working with a mixed group you should be prepared to join in as an equal member. I would go so far as suggesting that, when you come to performing, you take the principal role of the hero, with other group members taking other short scenes with you, though I did always find it easier to do all the stage management and have another colleague taking the main and pivotal role.

It is also a good idea to pair up for the exercises. After a while, stop and then allow everyone to tell his or her own story. At the end of this process you should have a crazy but original scenario for your show.

The storyline (see Fig. 41a)

Birgit, wheeling along, meets the King. He wants her chair, so he spreads his gold flowers all around for her to walk on instead. He gets into the chair and it tears away like a motorbike. The carpet of gold flowers becomes a magic carpet that flies her along, making her crash into Boris the Bad. The carpet wraps around his head and changes into a parachute. As he sails down, he spies Gretel the Girl skipping along below him—he's nasty, he swoops down, and tries to kiss her. She smacks him with her spanner because she wants nothing to do with him, and she changes his wand into a feather duster and her spanner becomes a motorbike and she zooms away. Boris the Bad finds he can't fly any more, because his magic wand is now a feather duster, so he walks along trying to find a job as a cleaner.

They then carry on travelling until the next encounter. What has happened to Birgit? Find a way to make her *active*. You will also have the following information after making a storyboard:

1 You will know what each character has to do, and you will find that the plot is based on *action*; which is much better for puppets than depending on words.

2 The plot will consist of short concise scenes. You will need to do some work to make the story stick together and carry out the necessary cuts. Aim to create a finished piece of no more than 20 minutes with a large group, or five minutes with a small group.

3 You will know what kind of puppets to make: for example, if they have to handle props they will need to be glove puppets; if they stand around and talk and point, they could be rod puppets. Do not worry

if the puppets are not all the same type. The bigger the variety the better.

4 You will know what kind of stage to use.
5 You will know the character of the puppet very well— you will feel in control of the project. This is important for the group members who have special needs.

You will be able to create a safe framework within which every member will be able to think for him- or herself.

The next stage is to move off the page and make the puppets. Expect to make a substantial number of these yourself, or else have made them in advance, and do the previous exercise based on the existing puppets. It is not always appropriate for students with severe learning disabilities to make their own puppets. If the student does not have sophisticated symbolic understanding, then question the relevance of puppet making for them. The journey from bits and pieces of materials to the completed whole will not take place. The vision of the completed puppet, even if you have a prototype, will not lodge.

The following is a description of a failure of a project and it failed essentially because I used puppet making as a way in to puppetry, when what I should have gone for straight away were theatre and performance games, and invested time in making a set of puppets in advance myself. This is a conclusion I have come to over and over again, with many different groups, not just those with learning disabilities. Puppet making has very little to do with *puppet theatre* other than being a way in for those who are particularly stimulated by a craft activity. Someone has to make the puppets but who?

My project was designed to introduce puppetry to Gateway Clubs (see Figs 42, 43 and plate 17). I started by telling the whole group a story, during which I made *Gregory the Green Dragon* before their eyes, following their direction on numbers of legs, teeth and other features. This part

Fig. 42.

Toothache

wire wool hair

wire twist 'specs'

gather cloth around neck

dowelling glued into bath-sponge head

Granny is a dentist

① Make slit in bottom of bath sponge
② Glue, gather and tie cloth around dowling 'neck'
③ Glue 'neck' into sponge
④ Cut slit for puppeteer's arm
⑤ Glue on features
Use dish-wash brush as giant toothbrush.

Sugar and Spice Lady

① Glue on hat
② Draw on features
③ Fold each doily, cut tiny slit at centre, slide up handle of spoon, glue into place
④ Make two tape hands and stick in place

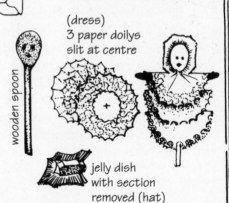

(dress)
3 paper doilys slit at centre

wooden spoon

jelly dish with section removed (hat)

Piece of black nylon stocking

Bacteria

① Knot stocking at top
② Stick self-adhesive cloth tape features onto stocking
③ Decorate with sequins
Wear as glove

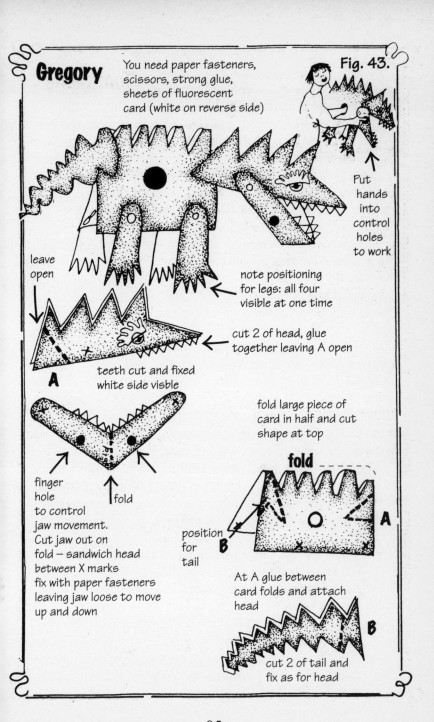

Gregory

You need paper fasteners, scissors, strong glue, sheets of fluorescent card (white on reverse side)

Fig. 43.

Put hands into control holes to work

leave open

note positioning for legs: all four visible at one time

cut 2 of head, glue together leaving A open

teeth cut and fixed white side visble

A

finger hole to control jaw movement. Cut jaw out on fold – sandwich head between X marks fix with paper fasteners leaving jaw loose to move up and down

fold large piece of card in half and cut shape at top

fold

position for tail

B

A

At A glue between card folds and attach head

B

cut 2 of tail and fix as for head

of the work always went well, because in a sense I was *'performing the making of a puppet'*.

Although I had introduced the characters from the play in the story, when I subsequently handed everyone their own little kit of varied and unusual materials, many participants could not see that they were making a puppet character. They just saw bits and pieces and not the whole. Parents and helpers took over and the puppet makers got bored and wandered away.

The actual performance later on in the evening took place after rounding up the cast, most of whom had drifted away as in their minds the project was over. However, I persuaded the *Sugar and Spice Ladies* to appear, on condition they were allowed to hold on to their shopping bags and handbags and keep their coats on, because they said that they were going home soon. *Gregory the Green Dragon* was steered on to stage and stayed there submissively until steered somewhere else. *Granny the Dentist* stood beaming, the *Bacterial* wriggled to order BUT NO OPERATORS SPOKE THROUGH OR IDENTIFIED WITH THE PUPPETS because no one had anything to say apart from me and my own big mouth.

My ideas were fine, but I should have focused much more clearly on the performance aspect of puppet theatre, working more appropriately on enabling the participants to identify with the puppet characters.

- There should have been more shorter sessions on the issues of the story (dental health), giving time for the participants to develop convictions of their own to be embodied by the puppets.
- I should have allowed more free play with the puppets so that the characters were completely familiar.
- And, finally, I should have explored physical movement with the participants to develop their understanding of puppet action.

Toothache was a project of twenty years ago. My ignorance about puppetry as a performing activity and my ill-placed emphasis on the craft aspect of it resulted from being a very new puppeteer. Since then there has been a massive increase in puppetry in education, and many more companies performing in schools. But, even recently, I advertised a performance workshop in schools for four to seven-year-olds, and a teacher still thought they should have made all the puppets which I took with me. There has to be less emphasis on making. The true benefits of puppetry are in the performance. So make your puppets in advance.

Starting to work with the puppets

- *Point out familiar features*: the puppet has eyes like me; he can look around like me; what can he see? He can move like me. (It can be difficult relating to body features if your client has a very uncertain body image. For example, working with a group of blind, year 7 children, even those with some sight had problems locating elbows and nostrils.) Developing body image and awareness is important.
- *Spend time on movement with your group in order to develop their own movement vocabulary.*
- *Explore action with your own bodies before working with the puppet.*

For example, recently a student from Israel, Vivien Waterman, was working on characterising the Polka by Shostakovich using animal puppets: the elephant, duck, frog and donkey. Before watching the puppets the children had a movement session with movement specialist and choreographer Wendy Cook, who helped them isolate different parts of the body in order to explore the animal characteristics: bottom wiggle for the duck; head for the donkey; knees for the frog; the back for the elephant. In this way the kinaesthetic sense of the children was thoroughly aroused and their physical perception of the characters enhanced for them to go on and use the puppets.

Using the puppets

To enable your group to understand that they can speak through the puppet and say anything they like, you have to set the example. You could make a collection of puppets (see Figs 44–47 and use them to retell actions and consequences).

- Choose a puppet yourself and keep the puppet 'in character' as long as possible while working with one other character operated by a member of the group. It is actually hard to improvise unless you have a particular gift for it so use the short sequences of movement below to start with (but allow freedom for any additional action/speech).

- At the end of each piece of action you should have established that when worked by a puppeteer the puppet 'comes alive', and when not being operated, it is just a doll. When you have had enough, put the puppet down, take your hand out of it. Keep reminding your puppeteers that the doll is just a doll, but when you have your hand inside you make the puppet come alive. This will seem obvious to you, but it is a message of empowerment to others.

- Enable each person to use the time when s/he is not operating to be an active audience member. They need to go through a routine of disengagement in order to move on and be able to make objective appraisals of the work they are watching.

   I was working in an inner city primary school behind Waterloo Station. As usual, I rehearsed the children in their parts with their marionettes,

rehearsed their going backstage—in fact every
moment of everything they did was rehearsed: 'the
picking up of the puppets', 'the putting down of the
puppets'. After the performance in the foyer of the
Queen Elizabeth Hall, we all said goodbye. I noticed
a dozen or so of them charging across the hall. They
skidded to a halt and without thinking all went into
the 'putting down of the puppets routine' and twelve
marionettes all lay neatly in a row as their owners
disappeared into the toilets.

Although it might seem a very controlled way of going
about things, I like to keep in mind the weaker members
of the group who need a framework in which to be free
to develop their creativity. It might be argued that such a
way of working is not playful because play by definition
is unstructured random activity. I would suggest that at
this stage it is game-type play and we are learning a few
rules to enable some to feel safe, and others to be able
to concentrate long enough to get something out of the
activity.

Useful actions and consequences

Fag Ash Lil sweeps the floor (Fig. 44)
*Fag Ash Lil sweeps the floor singing a sweeping song.
Every time she stops for a breather Maurice the Mouse
creeps in with some more rubbish. At first she thinks she's
just missed some, but then after two or three times she
gets suspicious. She hides and waits, and when she sees
Maurice the Mouse she jumps out and chases him away.*

Snappy Crocodile (Figs 45 and 46)
*Snappy Crocodile is lying in HIS river on a very hot day.
On one bank is a bottle of cola. On the other side is
Thirsty Jack.*

89

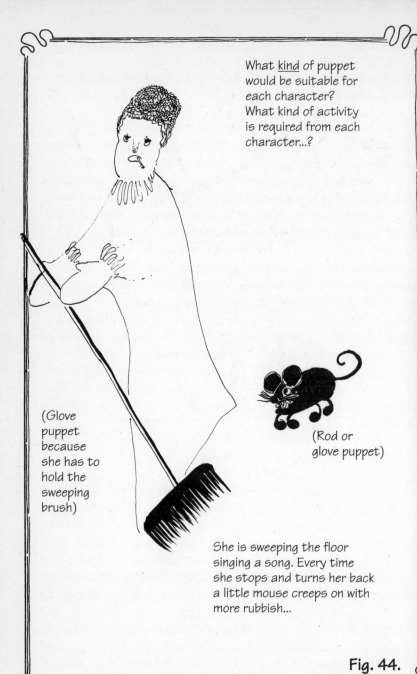

What <u>kind</u> of puppet would be suitable for each character? What kind of activity is required from each character...?

(Glove puppet because she has to hold the sweeping brush)

(Rod or glove puppet)

She is sweeping the floor singing a song. Every time she stops and turns her back a little mouse creeps on with more rubbish...

Fig. 44.

90

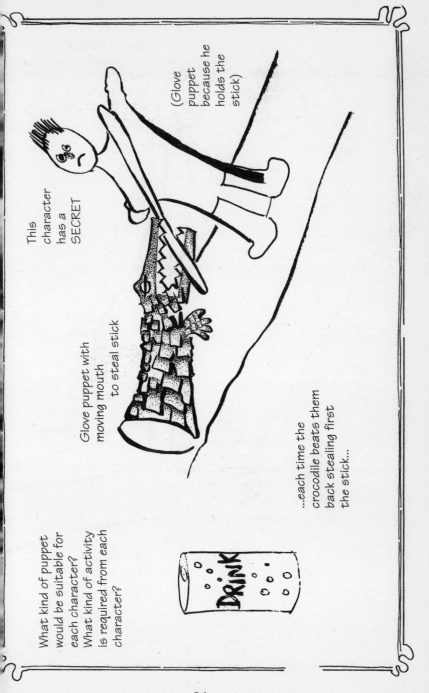

This character has a SECRET

(Glove puppet because he holds the stick)

Glove puppet with moving mouth to steal stick

...each time the crocodile beats them back stealing first the stick...

DRINK

What kind of puppet would be suitable for each character? What kind of activity is required from each character?

What kind of puppet
would be suitable
for each character?
What kind of activity
is required from each
character?

So he prays for the MAGIC
spell to work and...

...his legs grow and grow
and grow...
A SURPRISE!

Fig. 46.

What kind of puppet
would be suitable
for each character?
What kind of activity
is required from each
character?

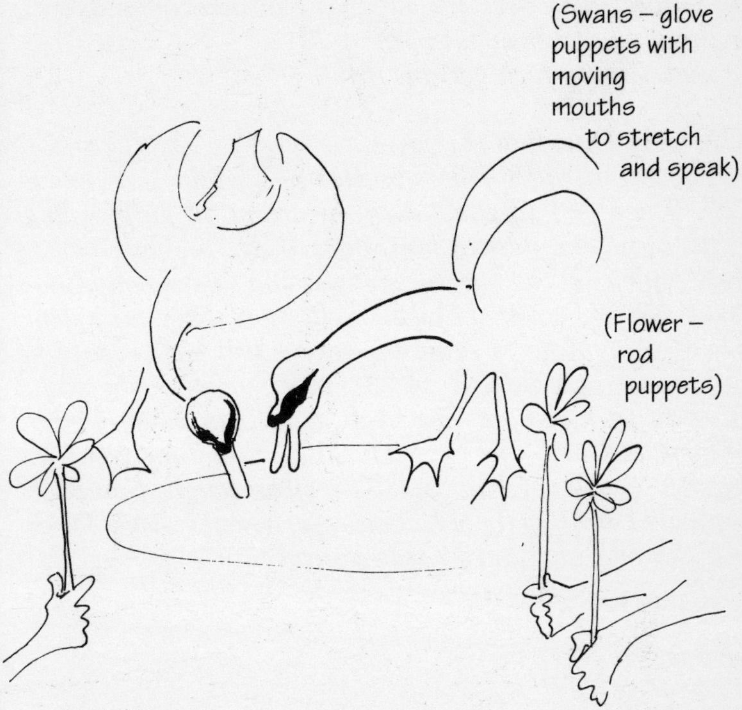

(Swans – glove
puppets with
moving
mouths
to stretch
and speak)

(Flower –
rod
puppets)

The swan tells him to look into
the water...

Fig. 47.

He has a net and a stick. He tries the stick to reach the
cola but the crocodile bites the stick and pulls it away. He
tries the net but after a lot of tangling and untangling the
crocodile gets that too. Finally, Thirsty Jack says a magic
word and then astonishingly his legs grow and grow until
he simply steps over the river and the crocodile can do
nothing whatever about it.

And Thirsty Jack gets his drink.

The Ugly Duckling (Fig. 47)
*His beautiful, fluffy yellow brother pecked the Ugly Duck-
ling. When he had gone away, his beautiful fluffy yellow
sister came and pecked him. Poor Ugly Duckling had to
leave, so he packed his little suitcase and swam away. Soon
it snowed and covered him all up like a blanket as he slept.
Then spring flowers came up but he still hid because he
knew how ugly he was and he didn't want the beautiful
swan to peck at him. The swan wanted to know why he
was hiding and the Ugly Duckling told him what his
brother and sister had said. The Swan laughed and told
the Ugly Duckling to look at his reflection. The Ugly Duckling did and saw that he was a swan too.*

Music

The use of music with puppetry is so natural. It can add
pace and variety to the performance and can provide emotional changes. (I used to play some 'repentance music' on
my mouth organ for Mister Punch after he killed Judy).

Puppets are N O T reality so you should feel free to break
into song whenever you like. Some of the very first puppetry I saw, which, at the time, I found inspiring, were
the Musical Turns devised by the Little Angel Marionette
Company. The same company has created *A Soldier's Tale*
by Stravinsky, *Reynard the Fox*, *Geneviève de Brabant* by

Satie, *Philomen and Baucis* by Hadyn and other whole operas. Opera heightens reality leaving it open most effectively to puppet play.

On a personal note, I was involved with much smaller-scale work. The puppeteer Walter Wilkinson, who according to his books seemed to sing throughout his glove puppet shows, was one example. As a new puppeteer, I thought it was the way things were done. After performing for a while, outside, in the open air, I realised that singing carries better over distance. Also the repetition of simple songs enables the audience to catch on to the essential facts about plot and character. When performing with people who have particular special needs, I always found it interesting that the children could never remember their lessons, yet they knew the latest pop music off by heart.

I made up very simple songs to sing throughout my own shows, e.g. 'The King's song':

All I want is more gold more gold more gold
All I want is more gold more gold mo-re gold.

Or Peter's song:

Gunga gunga gunga gunga
Gunga gunga gunga gunga.

Or Gretel's song:

A kiss for you
A kiss for me
A kiss for you
A kiss for me.

Songs can 'happen' during a practice or rehearsal period. I was recently working with some young children and we had a puppet character called Abimelech. After a few run-throughs, the child playing the part made the name into a kind of Aboriginal chant—a kind of 'Rolf Harris' parody.

Aaah
bimelech
aabim elech
aabim elech
aabim

Aaah
bimelech
aabim elech
aabim elech
aabim.

Short pieces of music are useful—whole songs or records are usually too long. You should be looking for seconds rather than minutes. A student showed me a piece of her work once, prior to training, and in it she had puppets dancing around to a complete Spice Girls record. She could have made her dramatic point with just a few seconds. Music written for dance is usually promising.

Live music accompaniment—such as percussion is excellent for all audiences, including those with special needs. From the educational point of view, accompanying helps to focus the participant. I usually have a particular instrument for a particular puppet character, for example: little bells for butterflies, a flexitone for the witch. There is a fantastic range of percussion instruments available now, and participants can make some of their own. Of course, accompaniment could be with any instrument.

Around my neck while I performed I wore: a mouth organ, a kazoo, a bicycle bell and a car horn. With me in the booth I also had a large cymbal on a stand with a foot pedal. I don't recommend all this—because I could not vouch for the quality of the puppetry.

Collaborations

Although it has to be argued that all theatre work is collaborative, puppetry has been until quite recently left on the sidelines. Currently, there is an increasing interest in using puppetry and object animation in visual theatre, and this has spilled out into education work rooted in some of the larger and more prestigious arts organisations. The projects I shall describe later in this chapter were by the National Youth Theatre and the Royal Opera House. You will notice that there is a strong musical element to these projects. Music and puppetry go well together. There are two ways of working collaboratively. The *multidisciplinary* approach—the different artform practitioners might have their own specific roles, and although there is a kind of working together, the different artists remain relatively uninformed personally about their different personal work processes.

Another method of working one might call *interdisciplinary* is for a group of artists to work together and to devise a work from what happens during their collaboration. This can be an exciting, compelling way of working; it involves risk-taking and is exhausting.

One piece of work I made was the outcome of working with a photographer, a dancer, a choreographer and a sound artist. I designed the set and costume, made the puppets and operated them, as well as playing the part of the Mother. Puppets and objects represented my 'child' and a group of villagers. The ideas we 'played with' were bereavement, mother and child relationships, mother and God relationships, marriage, weddings and funerals.

The dancer and choreographer came up with a graveside

dance for me to perform with an ironing board. I also had a dance with a sweeping brush. The 'villagers' were washing on the line and figures haunting the Mother. The photographer provided me with a series of 'pietà' images to describe the mother/child/ideas. And the sound artist put together my ideas for the script onto an audio tape that represented 'the thoughts of the mother' throughout the performance.

Often, devised work can be full of surprises, because, although you might know your collaborators well, there is the mix of media that creates all kinds of interesting and unusual juxtapositions. One London School of Puppetry student made a work from her collaboration with a poet, a choreographer, an earthquake scientist and herself as a puppeteer on another occasion, I was asked to go and add puppetry skills to a strange dance piece which included a naked woman lying in a bath full of water and orange plastic lobsters!

A project with the Britten Sinfonia involved several primary schools working with a poet to write their work, then with a composer to create an opera, then with a puppeteer, a choreographer, a director and an opera singer to create the performance.

Anyone can find it stimulating and exciting to move away from script-based presentation and be forced to create everything from scratch. It does, however, depend on confident leadership, knowledge of theatre and teaching strategies that leave people free to pitch in without feeling stressed (not having a ready-made script to rely on). Often a starting point might be to:

- design a set, or environment that informs and limits the millions of possibilities
- create an appropriate dramatic structure to the story: episodic, climactic.

There is not the space here to discuss this kind of work more fully, but giving space for every individual to explore and create is demanding and rewarding.

The following project takes a conventional approach with book and music for the show ready for interpretation.

Brilliant the Dinosaur by Richard Stilgoe was presented by the NYMT at the Edinburgh Festival. There were three of the dinosaur puppets for the production: a shadow puppet of a diplodocus; a large head with a moving mouth, and the complete puppet, being about forty metres long, that needed control rods for forty local children. They sat in the back row of the theatre with the puppet like a gigantic duvet concealed along the row at their feet. Very quietly on cue they would all get up together, walk into their position with the puppet raised and waiting until the lights were on it before processing, singing and operating as they went. The shadow puppet sequence of a dinosaur running, swimming in a storm and being chased by a crowd was strongly visual, but its effectiveness came out of the mixture of human movement, puppet images and storm lighting effects in dramatic collage.

The dinosaur has another appearance as a large lip-sync head in a cave to which the children in the cast have to respond. Once again, the scene only worked because of the mixture of human and puppet movement.

The piece was originally designed for three times that many children, and the plan was to keep them occupied in coaches and buses until close to their cue. (A questionable solution.)

When designing projects for children for whom theatre is a novel experience it is important to consider the balance between the length of time they are on stage and the length of time they are off stage. Wendy Cook, the director of the piece keeps the children in view of the stage, or actually on stage all the time, so that they are involved and interested throughout.

The Royal Opera House project was for local Bromley schools to perform at the Churchill Theatre, Bromley. A puppet sequence was designed for one school only. As the theatre is very large, small puppets would not have been appropriate. I designed five large lizard-type figures three metres long and two and a half metres high, each needing six operators, one on the head, one on each hand, one on each leg and one on the tail. The puppets were designed for performance under black or UV light, meaning that the children dressed from head to toe in black would not be visible.

The children were very lively eight-year-olds. With their teacher they did a technology project on joints. I built the puppets with them after showing them a smaller working model. They made the heads with moving jaws and made the hands and feet. I completed the bodies at the school so that the children were still involved and came in when they could to help. Fortunately the school had a dedicated art room so the figures could hang up drying and in a sense be on exhibition throughout the making period. As the children had made the heads, hands and feet themselves, they recognised their own work and were very proud of it.

The most enormous challenge came to these children when learning to operate their puppets, and special time had to be given over to this. Wendy Cook, the director and choreographer on this project, used movement exercises for them to explore co-operative movement in their own bodies first and found the children a lively and creative bunch.

Each group had to work as a team, so that the limbs, head and tail were all synchronised. I took the children down to the hall and we devised sequences of movement by counting. There were tremendous squabbles at first as they tried to co-ordinate—most of the boys wanted to be leaders, and only the girls had any concept of teamwork.

Backstage, the puppets had special 'parking places' so that they were ready to be picked up. The picking up of the puppets was rehearsed as carefully as what they were doing on stage. Once on stage in the dark the children galloped their monsters across, well ahead of the music. The children were dressed in black tracksuits and masks. My dressing in black and walking with them, to keep their pace even, solved this.

The children did some stunning collaborative work. On the Saturday a number of them failed to turn up for the performance because parents would not bring them. I expected to see some pretty rough operating, but as I ushered them on to the stage, every puppet seemed to have the correct number of operators. The children were thrilled with themselves because without telling me they had organised for puppeteers from previous puppets to run back round to the entrance side and pick up the operatorless limbs of the next puppets to take them over the stage as rehearsed. They had become superb team players through participating in this project.

A project like this is very worthwhile but the following points are worth noting:

(a) For large puppets you need space for storage and space backstage so that the puppeteers can easily pick them up. All backstage work needs to be rehearsed as much as on stage work.

(b) Physical movement should represent a proportion of the rehearsal time, so that the children develop their kinaesthetic sense, and fill their memories with the weight, timing and flow of the appropriate movement.

(c) Teamwork games can be played as part of the rehearsal time.

(d) Puppets are tiring.

(e) Every team needs a leader who is on the head of the puppet.

(f) It is not necessary for the children to make everything—but rather that there is a collaboration between the artist and the children and that significant parts such as the heads and hands and feet be made by the children.

(g) When children are working puppets they have no idea of what they look like. Take turns to let them watch each other. Just for fun at the theatre, the stage staff acted with the puppets a hilarious spoof and gave the children huge pleasure. It is an idea to take photographs and video what the children are doing to show them later.

You will note that the need for appropriate methods of rehearsal and the design of child-friendly work is emerging. All of these projects have involved paying-audiences in a professional theatre with professional artists, bringing a richness to the experience of the young people and their community alike.

Through projects like these, children learn self-discipline and enjoy a huge sense of achievement; their self-esteem is raised, their ability to focus, concentrate and to remain alert is enhanced. A large project can usually include young people with disabilities integrated into the rest of the cast. However, the sense of let-down and anticlimax after a positive experience could be a problem for young people with special needs. Therefore, it is important that teachers and carers monitor the progress of their charges in such projects, especially when they take place out of school time. They need someone with whom they can share their achievement when they go back into normal school life. Then their general schoolwork can properly benefit from the experience.

Section 2

For many people the puppet is only a craft object to be kept and admired. There *are* craft implications and they relate to making a figure robust enough to endure experimentation, rehearsal and repeated performance to an audience. The puppet is additionally an art object and the result of the impulse in every human being to respond to objects as if they are alive (whether by operating them or by participating as a spectator). Without a performance, we are dealing with something of unachieved potential—a might-have-been. Usually it is the fear of the therapist or teacher preventing the use of the puppet.

Section 3

The puppet as surrogate
Giving the surrogate a character
Developing the relationship with puppet
  and audience
Dealing with all that is horrible
The subversive puppet
Humour and the uses of subversion
Puppetry and therapy in child abuse

The puppet as surrogate

'With the emphasis on gesture and action, one began to get a double image of what was hailed as the ultimate in art: the picture and behind it the artist like some gesticulating ghostly presence.' Stuart Brisely, performance artist

Perhaps it should be made clear that someone does not become a puppeteer because s/he wants to be invisible or to disappear like some kind of neutral blob behind the puppet. The puppeteer has as strong a desire to be known as any other performer. Stuart Brisely made the statement above at a time in art history when artists wanted to be acknowledged *as they made their work*. It is peculiarly apt for me writing *I Am The Story*, for making one's presence known is what I would hope for all my clients. Puppetry is an art form that gives a voice and a language to those who perhaps have little voice. Behind every puppet is the *gesticulating, ghostly presence* of the puppeteer—through every puppet we glimpse the ever-present puppeteer.

The principal feature of puppetry that gives the puppeteer his or her voice is its *self-reflexivity*. The puppeteer makes a gesture and it is completed in the puppet: the puppet is the physical presence of the puppeteer, and always indicates the presence of the puppeteer either by their appearing together, or by showing the presence of the puppeteer through the puppet controls (see Fig. 4). Sometimes the presence of the puppeteer is easy to see, because he or she is visible; sometimes the puppeteer is

107

hidden away inside the stage, so you cannot see him or her. *But the presence of the puppet advertises the presence of the puppeteer somewhere.*

In *The Rescuers*, a Walt Disney cartoon, Penny the orphan child, clinging on to her Teddy is told that she must go down a deep, black hole in the ground to look for a hidden diamond. Tearfully, she tries to excuse herself by telling her captors that Teddy is afraid of deep, black holes. Teddy is taken away from her and she is told that she will never see Teddy again if she does not do as she's told. She goes down the hole, first telling Teddy not to worry about anything. She is going to be brave *for* Teddy.

This is an illustration of the use of the surrogate. The individual has the ability to transfer fears and hopes into a beloved object. The puppet object becomes a bridge between the inner fantasy life and the outer world of reality. This object makes life bearable by providing a temporary or transitional place of safety while the potential of new situations is being considered.

A feature of surrogacy in puppetry is that there could be many characters—one puppeteer might play several parts simultaneously—such as in Punch and Judy, or as in most folk hand-puppet shows. There can also be many fragments—often in more complex professional shows, several puppeteers might operate one puppet—taking, for example, a hand each, or the head and the feet, such as in the Bunraku Theatre of Japan (see Fig. 48), and having to move as one (see plate 13). Some puppets in film might need five puppeteers to work the facial features alone. In therapeutic work, I have often used puppet types that require several operators, in order to develop less confident participants, perhaps to be able to manipulate very large puppets. The result is some excellent teamwork and less able children can rise to an enormous challenge. The puppet, fragments, or large casts of puppets all act in the same way, by working transitionally in the life of the person.

Fig. 48.

Japanese Bunraku Puppet

One puppet has more than one operator –
imagine in your own situation how one person's
confidence and ability to communicate could be
increased by working alongside someone
more experienced ...

The inner world of the imagination is where the character of the puppet originates. The outer and real world is not where the object is played with, because the world of art is not the real, everyday world. The performance place is a kind of fantasy playground for the puppet.

Social workers using anatomically correct dolls, in an effort to get disclosures of sexual abuse from children, made a mistake by assuming the play/art world of dolls was the real world of actual experience. The individual using puppets therapeutically can only hint at real experience. The puppet is being used to hold on to a sense of cohesion and control. Penny in *The Rescuers* can only keep her head in the real world by pretending she is caring for Teddy in her fantasy world. In fact, it is the idea of the controlling presence of the puppeteer that has given us so much imagery about power and powerlessness: puppet state; puppet leader; just a puppet on a string and others.

This fantasy/reality dichotomy will be discussed later in the section, 'Puppetry and therapy in child abuse'.

Giving the surrogate a character

We start to use surrogacy as an infant when we have to cope with separation from the mother we had been so physically attached to in the womb that we might have thought that I and mother and mother and I were ONE. After birth, I, the crying baby, am pacified, and oneness is achieved briefly at feeding times. In between, the dawning aloneness has to be dealt with by the first social and creative act of my life—I choose a temporary replacement for my mother, one of many in fact: perhaps my fingers, the dummy, the corner of the blanket, a toy, and everyone else agrees and helps me to get this replacement. A way of dealing with aloneness is to take on a surrogate; to try out difference; or, to try out different aspects of the individual

110

in the world—in other words, to rehearse the possible before the real thing has to happen.

In order to achieve a collective connectedness throughout life, the choice of a surrogate is crucial. However, it is worth remembering that disability of any kind might prevent the actual operation of the puppet, but need not prevent empathy with the surrogates (puppets) from within an audience. Think of the puppet as a bridge, with the energy of the audience and of the puppeteer passing in both directions. Through the puppet it is possible to reach backwards and even return in memory and fantasy to childhood or another period of life to view it from a different perspective, perhaps to reassess it or simply to enjoy it again.

When using a puppet you are capitalising on an inborn response to animate an object.

Exercises

Read through the following:

1 Take a puppet, name it, give it some interesting likes and dislikes
2 Introduce it to a child or children who are experiencing difficulties of some sort.
3 Answer the questions (see below).

The following comments were made by a speech therapist: basing her work on 'Hilary' see Fig. 56 and plate 7.

I was particularly interested by the way you used a puppet to be alongside a child doing a difficult or potentially boring bit of work, to gain a better response. I tried this with a sleeve puppet, which I'd already used in some sessions, a caterpillar called Henry. I've started using him regularly with certain children, watching what they're doing, inspecting their work and copying from them. I've also tried to develop his personality and looks—he wears

111

glasses for reading—and I found that children respond with more interest and spontaneous backchat. A little boy asked Henry if he'd noticed anything different about him that morning! He'd had a haircut. The whole thing is great fun . . .'

Analysis
We could analyse the above situation in terms of the little boy and Henry the Caterpillar to see if there is the potential for communication through puppetry. I am using a standard framework I have developed for use in my work to evaluate what is happening.

1 *Q*. What kind of relationship does the little boy have with the puppet—is he engaged as a spectator or as a puppet operator?
   A. Apparently as participant spectator.
2 *Q*. Once engaged in either role, is there a desire to give in to social expectations by responding to the audience, or is he in the audience responding directly to the puppet?
   A. The little boy has made friends with the puppet.
3 *Q*. Is there a clear desire to use the puppet to communicate to spectators?
   A. First thing in the morning and the little boy talked to Henry, who was being operated by the speech therapist. There was clearly a need to talk (perform).
4 *Q*. Is there the ability to distinguish between doll play that does not need an audience and puppet play that does?
   A. Yes, in this study it is an audience occasion (other children around) with certain expectations.
5 *Q*. Are puppets being used to extend social repertoire, communication, intellectual content, expression of feelings, making moral choices?
   A. Yes, in this case the boy spoke spontaneously to

the puppet about something he thought might interest the puppet—Obviously very satisfactory for the speech therapist.

6 Q. How appropriate is the action for the character depicted by the puppet?

A. The little boy was treating the puppet as a friend to whom he might say anything. The scene was set up for this purpose.

7 Q. Is your client able to play jokes with the puppets— to play with the ridiculous, the unexpected?

A. This is yet to develop.

Developing the relationship with puppet and audience

As we have seen above an early objective in puppetry is to enable a person to relate to the puppet, in other words, to make friends, or, at a later date, to be able to respond appropriately to the type of character s/he is meeting. Below, I have the transcript of a conversation I have had with one of my puppets and an audience, including someone called John who does not speak out loud. You will notice that, as a performer, I want John and the other children to get to know Tubby and all his little ways—I make up stories around him and with him so that, just as in the illustration by the speech therapist above, there will be spontaneous talk between the children and the puppet (see Figs 49, 50 and plate 4).

Dual Control Puppet

Fig. 49.

one person
may work
one rod

sleeves
gathered

one person
works the
arm tubes

diagram
to show how
puppet may
be worked
by more
than one
person

back view

head (foam type, see
instructions in fig. 52)

foam hands
(see instructions
in Fig. 16b)

child's large
shirt

sew at
waist

child's trousers

child's boots
or shoes
(see Fig. 16c)

114

Fig. 50.

A Character: Tubby...

(dual control puppet)

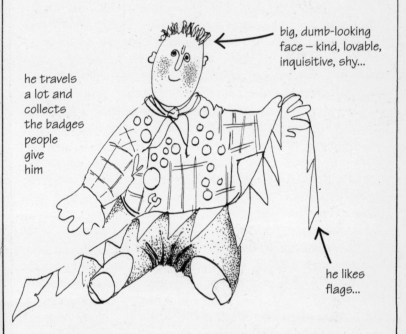

big, dumb-looking
face – kind, lovable,
inquisitive, shy...

he travels
a lot and
collects
the badges
people
give
him

he likes
flags...

He also has in his pocket; a puppet frog, tadpole,
spider, a peanut, a balloon, a clockwork gorilla and
a picture of a witch painted by a boy who had
been in the audience –
It is important to make every puppet special
by adding different details to show his character.
Details can be added and the puppet completed
as a group activity...

'This is my friend Tubby. Say hello Tubby. Yes, more
people. Whenever he comes out of his case' (the children
need to understand that puppets are puppets and only
come to life when they want them to—they are not living
things being smothered to death in plastic bags and suit-
cases) 'there are more people here! Shall we look at him?
Yes, he's fat, isn't he? Can you guess what he collects?
Yes, badges—he collects badges. He's got them all over
his shirt, hasn't he? What does this one say on it? THE
GREAT MILK RUSH—that's to remind him to drink
milk. Actually he doesn't drink milk because puppets don't
need to drink or eat anything.' (Another reminder that
puppets are not real, living things but part of a game we
are playing together) '. . . Are you wearing the badge to
remind everyone else to drink milk Tubby? Yes. I like
milk—do you? Here's another badge—it says MY
NAME'S TUBBY—yes, that's your name—What's your
name? It's John? Right—well we're very pleased to meet
you—aren't we Tubby. Yes, let's shake hands. No you
can't all shake hands with Tubby—why not all shake
hands with each other.' (At this point the children have
become very excited, so I need to calm them down) 'Do
you want to know a secret? Be very quiet then because
I'll have to whisper it. This old squidgy balloon here is
full of Canadian air! What do you think of that? Here we
are in Milton Keynes, in your school and Tubby has a
balloon full of Canadian air! That's because we've been
on holiday there visiting friends . . . and guess what else
there is in his pocket—do you want to show them Tubby?
What was that? They mustn't touch? I shouldn't think
they'd want to touch it . . . it's a horrible gooey Canadian
toffee. What else is there in his pocket—Oh no! a wiggly
tadpole . . . ooooh and a squiggly spider . . . and a toy
gorilla—and what's this? A hanky? No . . . it's a flag . . .
it's lots and lots of flags!'

The puppet is being seen in relation to the puppeteer. This is how the children are learning about the character of Tubby by watching how he behaves with his operator. The relationship is a play relationship. The puppeteer has a special kind of glove puppet who has a name and does naughty things like hiding sticky old sweets in his pocket. They were both sharing with everyone else in the audience so that everyone could see the badges and the tadpole and spider.

The next conversation is with a puppet of a different type and personality. I call this kind of puppet 'a dual control'. I have found it useful as a means of encouraging clients who are poorly motivated, or fearful, or who avoid eye contact as with autism. I can sit alongside the operator and we share the working of the puppet. At first it might be myself taking 99 per cent of the work, working the head rod and one hand, with my assistant working the other hand—but gradually, as confidence is increased, the energy from my client increases, until he or she is taking over.

Ted is a very tall rod puppet (Figs 51 and 52). What can you tell about him from the following conversation?

'Hello this is Ted. Ted doesn't speak. I've brought him along because he says he's worried. Do you know what he's worried about? He's worried about what goes on behind all these closed doors, inside all these little rooms. What do you do in these little rooms? I told him I'd show him one day and he's worried and worried so now I've brought him to see you ... and now he's met you he's nervous—Oh Ted, you don't have to hide your face— these children don't want to hurt you—Can you all say "don't worry" to Ted for me? There you see Ted, don't cry, here's your hanky—blow your nose—what an enormous blow—it sounded like a fog horn!' (The funny noise has made everyone excited so they need to be calmed down.) *'Ted is so tall that some people are afraid of him—but we*

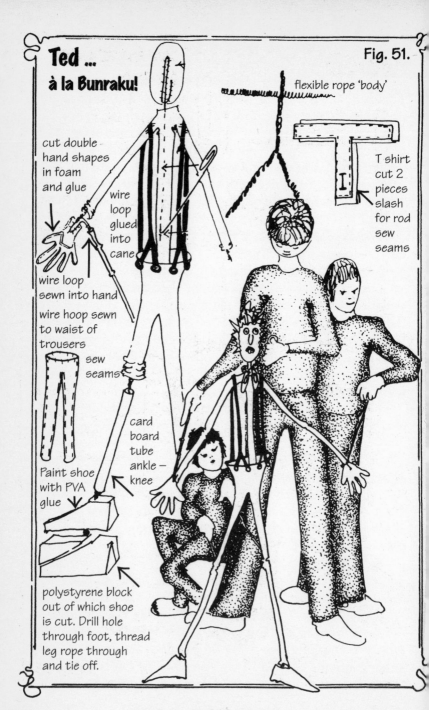

Ted ...
à la Bunraku!

Fig. 51.

flexible rope 'body'

cut double
hand shapes
in foam
and glue

wire
loop
glued
into
cane

T shirt
cut 2
pieces
slash
for rod
sew
seams

wire loop
sewn into hand

wire hoop sewn
to waist of
trousers

sew
seams

card
board
tube
ankle –
knee

Paint shoe
with PVA
glue

polystyrene block
out of which shoe
is cut. Drill hole
through foot, thread
leg rope through
and tie off.

118

Ted cont...

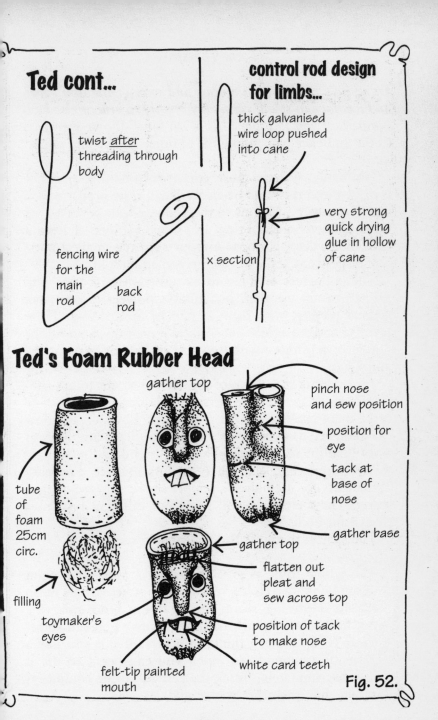

twist _after_ threading through body

fencing wire for the main rod

back rod

control rod design for limbs...

thick galvanised wire loop pushed into cane

very strong quick drying glue in hollow of cane

x section

Ted's Foam Rubber Head

gather top

pinch nose and sew position

position for eye

tack at base of nose

gather base

tube of foam 25cm circ.

filling

toymaker's eyes

gather top

flatten out pleat and sew across top

position of tack to make nose

white card teeth

felt-tip painted mouth

Fig. 52.

119

*know he's really very nervous and very gentle don't we?
and we have to speak very, very quietly to him or else he'll
jump. Can you whisper "hello" to him?'* (Some members
of the audience will choose the option to make him jump.)

Gradually, even the most reticent person in the audience
is drawn into this kind of scene. There is no pressure, you
see. The direct questions to the audience can be answered
or not. Sometimes I bring an animal puppet—I have a
hedgehog asleep in a box. A request for the smallest possible response is actually often returned tenfold.

The puppeteer only has to hint at something 'real' and
the spectators use their imaginative powers to construct
the full picture, with them as part of that picture. There
is the unspoken agreement to form a relationship with the
puppet as a bridge—with two-way trafficking of emotions
and ideas.

Also note that the aim of the activity is not to get children over-excited. I have introduced common strategies to
bring them back down. It is important, however, to allow
the audience to experience a variety of highs and lows of
emotional intensity. Panto Philpott, friend and mentor of
many puppeteers, said that there are three necessary
ingredients for a children's puppet show: surprise, magic,
secret. These elements will bring out different responses
from your audience.

The speech therapist had a further comment:

The whole thing is great fun—but I take your point
about 'making a child excited does not necessarily mean
that he is learning' so am bearing this in mind and trying
not to lose sight of my treatment aims . . . It can sometimes be a failing, I think, in a therapist, if you like a
piece of equipment so much you can begin to use it
less discriminately, fitting the activity to the equipment
rather than the other way round . . .

This last section on the character was to get you going with your first 'solo' character, so that you experience working through a surrogate—your puppet. We are now going on to explore more of the nature of the puppet. It is very important to build on the idea of the puppet being a separate being—we know it is under our control or under the control of the puppeteer, but the game of puppetry is to pretend that it is separate from you. Claire, in the Hilary the Witch episode (see p. 13) was very careful to make sure that the character was actually a puppet and not a real witch. Puppet means control—but the pretence is that we can do our own thing through the puppet and EVERY-ONE PRETENDS IT'S THE PUPPET.

Dealing with all that is horrible

The illustrations above represent some quite light-hearted uses of surrogacy to enable you to understand how it feels to work through a surrogate and to give you confidence to handle others responding to you. But the use of a puppet to carry great pain or to explore evil in the life of a person is obviously also possible. In recent activity with very young children I used the following dramatic devices in a performance workshop. It was based on the work of Ann Campion, a nurse working with children and their families.

I told a story to the children about a wood, near which a child and mother lived. In the wood was a 'magic cauldron'. I tried out different names for this object—like 'hot pot', but all my groups of children preferred the mystery of the cauldron. I had painted it bright pink and covered it with sequins and the children told me that it was not a witch's cauldron nor was it a bad thing. I told the children that it was full of good things and that if you drank from it you would be strong and happy. I asked the children what they would put into it. The following is a typical list:

Kittens
Puppies
Kisses
Ice cream
Biscuits
Smiles
Tractors
Fire engines
Dairy products (a recent project)
Onomatopaeia (even the teacher was impressed!)

We then pretended to put them into the cauldron, and then we passed it around and took a drink. We pretended the drink had a flavour—everyone found their own flavours and added a bit of a fizz here and there. As the children became freer and more relaxed—the effect of the 'drink' was very amusing—the children smiled or showed me their new muscles and they all talked about being strong and happy. We established the force of 'good'. I continued with the story.

Also in the wood was the Tree of Horribleness. This was a dreadful black and sparkling green creation made from a large dustbin. It grew from all the horrible things in the world—all the rubbish in the world. I asked the children what sort of things are the horrible things:

Witches
Ghosts
Foot and mouth
Chickenpox
Blood (?)
Bats (?)
Snakes
Bullies
People who hurt people

We then disposed of all these nasty things by putting them into the roots of the tree; in this way we located the force of 'evil'. Some children took the branches and made it grow bigger, two children took the trunk of the tree and made it rumble. It needed a victim, who had *not* drunk from the cauldron, but everyone had, and the tree shrunk down again.

These two things then were part of a story in which the choice was to drink from the cauldron and be strong and happy, or become the victim of the Tree of Horribleness. The child who did not drink had to be rescued from the Tree by the Mother who flew in just in time.

It is important that Good and Evil are not equally opposing forces. There has to be an overcomer more powerful than all the good and all the evil—like the Mother in this story and Rubber in Meena Naik's work (see p. 131). Children need a way to deal with evil and disappointment; they also need to have a clear idea of who and what is wrong—especially if they were ever to become victims. Meena Naik makes an interesting depiction of evil in her play about Aids—Aidus is both attractive and horribly wicked. The challenge in her work is to persuade the young girls that sex has an evil aspect they have to combat in order to survive. Having a clear concept of evil means that to some extent fear of life in general can also be minimised.

Play specialists working in hospital aim to reduce fear through play with puppets, because fear blocks understanding. The idea is that a patient is able to confront the terrible experiences he or she has to go through by means of various strategies using puppets. These are essentially ways of getting information to the child about what is going to happen to him or her. Some children will block off or refuse to have anything to do with the information, and many adults find it equally dreadful to talk about what their child is going to have to go through. The other use the puppet has in hospital is therapeutic, enabling the child to use fantasy as a means of survival.

Some hospitals use male and female anatomical puppets that fascinate the children (and repel many adults). They have a complete set of organs, bones, tonsils, brain, genitalia, and the skin can be unzipped and the organs removed (obviously with timing and sensitivity). The child, working with one of these puppets and a specialist, will enable the specialist to note how much the child understands, what words he or she is using, and what kind of fears he has.

A play-specialist was working with a thirteen-year-old boy with learning disabilities. He played with the puppet-patient, with himself acting the role of the surgeon, in the lead-up to his own operation. He told the puppet that his 'willy had now been chopped off'. Through repeated play sessions, the specialist was able to introduce the correct information and allay fears in a less confusing non-verbal way.

When, during a training session, a group of teachers and therapists made a simple rod puppet using black polythene, some of them objected, saying that it was too frightening for them to use with children. We then went on to improvise with it in order to explore how children actually deal with what is horrible in their lives.

Puppeteer Bjorg Mykle was requested by a therapist to provide monster puppets (see plate 9) of ever-increasing nastiness for two reasons: to enable the child to tell the secret of his or her abuse, and to help the child cope with feelings of anger or grief. In the conference report, the following example was given:

> One little boy had witnessed the abuse and murder of his baby sister in the bathroom. He would not speak or enter a bathroom. In a therapy session, he covered a model bathroom with red paint, took a baby doll and

put it on to the toilet and told it to watch as he knotted the long rubber arm of the monster puppet and ran it under the boiling hot tap. The monster puppet then became his friend. He told the monster his secret and the monster was angry at adults mistreating children. The monster gave a hammer to the boy so that he could crush his bad dreams. This boy did recover quite significantly as a result of this therapy.

Another example of 'monster therapy' was with a five-year-old Danish boy who showed signs of abuse:

He played with the monster puppet with the specialist operating it. He gave the monster 'sleep food' which were perhaps sedative drugs, put pins in the monster and refused to tell the monster who was hurting him. He also put Plasticene 'excreta' into his mouth and told the therapist operating it to make the monster vomit it up. He then beat up and fought the monster. Finally the monster became his friend and he told it his story.

The monsters could represent the abuser, and revenge could be exacted. The monster could personify all the anger and pain of the child and, once these were externalised, the child was no longer fearful.

The subversive puppet

How is it that someone who is a victim can feel empowered by using a puppet? The whole concept of the puppet is the conflict between the controlled and the controller: master/servant; weak/strong. But what happens if the puppet takes over the puppeteer? The servant overcomes the master? The weak overcomes the strong? This must be appealing to someone who feels small and insignificant.

The puppeteer Henk Boerwinkle used to play a scene between two characters: his own puppeteer hands and a marionette, playing with the idea of the puppet being autonomous:

The marionette is tired of being under the control of the puppeteer and rebels. A tug of war between the hands and the puppet follows. In the end the hands relent and laying down the control beside the marionette the hands fall limp and lifeless—because there is no life for the puppeteer without the puppet. But, of course, the marionette is also lifeless, because there is no life for the puppet without the puppeteer. But, then, the trick. The marionette gets up all by itself (instead of being worked from above as a marionette, it is now being worked from below as a glove puppet). *It takes over the marionette control and hobbles off, using it as a crutch.*

As a boy puppeteer, Ronnie Le Drew described seeing a performance in what was Czechoslovakia. The scene is between a puppeteer and his rebellious marionette:

The marionette performance came to an end and the puppeteer was putting away the marionette. The marionette argues because he does not want to be put away into the bag, but he has to be. The bag is slung over the back of the puppeteer, but in the split second before applause, a voice shouts from the bag 'You can do what you like with me, but you can't stop me from thinking!'

Once we have grasped this idea and can play with the idea that the puppet is 'alive' and separate from us, we can then invest in it some of the things that frighten us. This last example was taken from a performance in a country under Soviet Communist control. In response to this, puppeteers began to perform visibly, operating their puppets in sight of the audience instead of hiding behind masking—inside a booth or behind a screen. They were taking the puppet as a metaphor for themselves under the control of the State, being dangled from strings by their leaders. They were using their puppets to disclose what they saw as the truth of Communism. But, by investing their fears in the puppet, they could play with ideas of freedom of thought and defy the State. One group operated their marionettes with very thick, highly visible strings, fearlessly allowing the puppets to demonstrate for them and their audiences how they saw their lives under Communist rule. As we have already seen, the transitional aspects of the puppet mean that audience and puppeteer are protected.

Humour and the uses of subversion

In the eighteenth century, Samuel Foote *and* his flat wooden cut-out puppets were arrested for vagrancy. The judge released the puppets because he said he could not pass judgement on objects and then he released Sam Foote because he had a wooden leg, which meant he was one quarter puppet. People have fun with the idea of the puppet. The magistrate was obviously having fun at the expense of the person who brought charges against Sam Foote.

Clearly, the use of humour is vital in many situations that are normally stressful. I once asked an occupational therapist what use she thought puppets were in her family therapy sessions—'they always make us laugh' she said, 'and some families haven't laughed together for years'.

Sidsel Berg, an occupational therapist, at one conference, described a case when a mother and son, Danny aged twelve, were admitted to the acute psychiatric ward. The problem was that the mother could not show any interest in her child or have confidence in his abilities. She was shy and withdrawn. As a result, the son had lost confidence in himself and avoided school for many months.

After playing out a discussion between two puppets, the son wrote up on a board: 'We shall play with puppets instead of human beings.' Danny directed three adults in improvised stories; with his mother, a nurse and Sidsel using ready-made puppets. At first, Danny tried to protect his mother from embarrassing herself by only letting her come on at the end and even then cut her short. However, she practised her slinky movements with a caterpillar puppet, lost her shyness and talked freely through the puppet. Danny pretended to be a TV reporter and asked for the scene to be videoed. He interviewed the puppets 'in a very serious way'. And then everyone watched the replay.

Having the opportunity to take charge gave Danny back some confidence and impressed his mother, but a major part of the therapy was the chance they had to laugh together. The son was happy to see his mother laughing and pleased at her abilities to perform.

'C', a London School of Puppetry student, discovered while studying that the comic aspects of a puppet were what freed her from a painful haunting. As she learnt to operate a very large five-foot-high witch-type character whom she called Nancy, she found she personified to her the 'critical parent figure'. This was a negative, blaming inner voice that had haunted 'C' and crippled her emotionally, and had always made her feel a complete failure. She developed a scenario in which Nancy the Witch representing the 'critical parent' went to a party expecting to impress everyone. Unexpectedly, she was only the wallflower, she flounced out and, instead of the frightening and intimidating figure she always had been in 'C's' imagination, collapsed pathetically, 'the epitome of collapsedness'. 'C' repeatedly performed this scenario to us until its humour was thoroughly explored and she was able to use the new inner image to encourage herself when about to succumb and turn into 'a sticky pool of despair'. The puppet had given her the space and lightheartedness to consider the potential of alternative situations.

Another image she found was a bird puppet image—we called it the Image of Freedom. In her imagination she saw herself as a rather beautiful but caged bird. She is an illustrator and depicts many such birds. 'C' led a puppet making session in which a large group of nearly thirty participants all made white birds. When completed, smiling and excited, we took the birds outside for their flight—and they became the images of freedom—from anything that holds us down and back.

Exercises

1 Imagine a really negative idea.
2 Personify, think of a character to depict the idea.
3 Draw, paint or make a puppet of it.

In two case studies, we shall see the idea of the puppet's surrogate characteristics giving freedom to people inhibited by despair. They need time and space to consider the potential in alternative situations.

Dr Santiranjan Paul and Meena Naik are working in India. Dr Paul is a GP from Calcutta and used puppetry in leprosy education; Meena Naik is an actor living and working in Bombay and uses puppets in various educational projects. Gary Friedman works in South Africa, also in education. All three have found that, by using puppets, the prejudices and fears of their participants can be relieved, and the message clearly seen and heard.

In Dr Paul's work with leprosy, his glove puppets are acceptable to Muslim, Hindu and Christian audiences, as are the slides and posters he also uses which carry more technical descriptions of the symptoms of the terrible disease.

In his performance, a promising young graduate loses a prospective job in the government because the medical officer discovers that he has leprosy. His family is hysterical because they believe that there is no cure and that the carrier of the disease has brought shame on the whole family who would all be shunned by society. Leprosy is a disease that is surrounded by superstition and social stigma. The young man has to face the prospect of banishment. However, since he is well educated and intelligent, he tells his mother not to worry, because the doctor has told him that there is treatment available. His mother, however, representing the voice of the people, does not believe him and prepares for the worst. He goes to the leprosy specialist and is cured.

In terms of education, what prevents learning is often a fear of change or a fear of unknown consequences. And yet we also know that the consequences of little education are horrifying. I remember talking to someone who was working for one of the charities in Africa. He told me that the key to the future prosperity of undeveloped countries lay in providing good water supplies and education for girls: the two elements were inseparable, but people, on the whole, were too afraid to educate girls.

Although we understand that the puppet is worked by the puppeteer and that union is never broken—one of the most exciting aspects of puppetry is the way it can be subverted: we are persuaded that the puppet is an autonomous being, giving the puppeteer freedom to say anything and the spectator freedom to hear anything because it is the puppet doing it—we are innocent bystanders.

It was a moving experience to watch Dr Paul's show, because it was clear that this old GP knows his audience and uses every means possible to dispel superstition and fear in his patients. His wife and family perform with him and help to make the puppets. Some years ago he won an award from Mother Teresa for his work.

Meena Naik was approached by Population Services International (PSI) to run an Aids Education project in Kamathipura, the red light district in the heart of Bombay. Unlike Dr Paul, as an actor and puppeteer she has no medical background and needed to research her work thoroughly before she could start the project. She was horrified at what she discovered. The sex-workers were voiceless victims, and social outcasts, many no more than children. They usually had homes in villages far away, to which they sent money—though the families would not know the nature of the work producing the pay. Half of the prostitute's money went to the brothel keepers. Ninety per cent of the illegitimate children of prostitutes become prostitutes too. The women are usually superstitious and selling themselves is seen as a service to the goddess Yellama.

Drink and violence in the men means that little care is taken in their handling of the sex-workers; rape, physical and drug abuse are common and use of condoms rare. The women are usually in poor health, and as social outcasts find it hard to get medical care. They resort to quacks and become the victims of unimaginably bad care with the risk of further infections from unsterilised equipment. Sex-workers with open wounds go on taking customers in unregistered and unchecked brothels.

Meena Naik was faced with enormous fear and prejudice from the sex-workers. She could not approach them directly because they were afraid of their pimps and brothel-owners, who would attack the women if they felt they were being drawn away from earning. From her understanding of puppets, she knew that to be the only way she could communicate with the girls. She knew that just as in the previous illustration concerning leprosy, puppetry is able to concretise abstractions, so that leprosy or

HIV, which in most of us are abstract fears, can be objectified and dealt with. Dr Paul used a more documentary approach—but depicting each character as a puppet makes an unthreatening representation of the fears of the spectator. Meena was much more theatrical in her approach: HIV became a tangible monster and the condom a saviour called Rubber, which drawing on Christian and Hindu mythology, looked and behaved like both Jesus Christ and the Lord Vishnu.

Her script was about Champabai the narrator, a new young sex-worker called Kamalabai, and Aidus who appears both as a monster and as a friendly person. Aidus persuades a customer of the prostitute to throw away his condom and Kamalabai to give herself a medical injection with a re-usable needle. She becomes infected. However, a heavenly character called Nirodh (Rubber) appears from the sky and convinces the customer, the doctor and Kamalabai of the wickedness of the monster Aidus and, hailing Rubber, they drive Aidus away.

Although at the Condom Festival (Masti Mela), the performance of the evening show was very successful and hundreds of condoms were sold to customers of the prostitutes, the young sex-workers were not there because they were working. Meena Naik decided to train the PSI workers to work directly with the girls, using a more secretive, unthreatening approach, with smaller puppets made from cigarette packets and matchboxes (see plate 18).

The PSI worker would sit in a bar or in the street talking to the girl or girls and tell the story of Aids using the puppets. The young prostitutes not only listened and watched, but they also became completely open about their lives as they spoke to the puppets or spoke through the puppets as they operated them themselves. The PSI workers were able to give advice to the girls and the names and addresses of legitimate doctors.

Puppeteer Gary Friedman's Aids Education project was run in a South African prison. Several puppetry and drama workshops enabled the prisoners to talk about their lives in the prison—particularly the corrupt system of bribes from older male prisoners to the warders to procure young boy prisoners for them. The puppetry enabled the young people to expose what was happening to them and the public performance gave them, as victims, a public voice.

Gary Friedman's work previously with African Research and Education through Puppetry Programme followed a similar theme—using puppets as a 'safe' voice for victims. One project was to use puppets on television to persuade women not to be afraid to register to vote in the first elections, to reassure them that their vote was free, and not be intimidated to vote as their husband or anyone else in power might tell them. But both he and Meena Naik felt that TV puppetry in a country with most of the population without television was limited and that the success of puppetry still lies in face to face live entertainment.

To end this section, it is useful to remember that ignorance takes a person's voice away from them. The puppet can give someone back their voice and their story along with it.

Exercises

1 Think of an issue affecting your group, e.g. eating junk food, smoking, etc.
2 Talk about it with the group.
3 Invent a very short dialogue between two puppets, make one character 'good' and the other 'bad' about the issue for the group to watch, then, after the performance of the scene, discuss the issue with them again.

4 Note how well the information has got over to them in each case. Invent a scene, but personify a central character very theatrically, show them the scene, then discuss it with them.

Puppetry and therapy in child abuse

At one of the London School of Puppetry conferences, we played host to Bjorg Mykle from Norway. One day as a teacher she was confronted with a withdrawn, aggressive, dirty little girl who asked the glove puppet if their heads hurt when their bare feet were in the snow. 'We don't have feet' replied the puppets. The little girl was immediately at ease and shared her secret: when drunk, her parents would throw her out into the snow. Talking to puppets can never be evidence, because it is play, but this play provided clues, which were then verified, and the child moved to foster parents.

Bjorg provided several institutions with puppets— attractive ones without mouths. The mouths could be added by the child as part of the therapeutic process of disclosing a repressed secret. The puppets were not specifically male or female, which meant that naming gender could be part of the empowering process of the child. Bjorg Mykle also uses very small puppets—only the height of the hand, which are less intimidating for children who fear being touched. Both Bjorg Mykle and Madge Bray, working with smaller children, recommend playing with the puppets on the floor as a way of inviting children to join them. Priority in this work is to make the child feel as much at ease as possible, so that the therapeutic value of telling the secret which was eating away at him or her can be facilitated, whether it is a case of diagnosis or of police evidence.

Bjorg wrote in her notes for the conference:

For small children it is nearly impossible to talk about bad secrets. When it comes to incest, a child will most often be crushed in dilemmas: his or her agony versus loyalty towards the abuser. A child's most effective language is metaphoric play. This play might allow the therapist to take part in the child's inner landscape and find out what the child is trying so very hard to tell. Puppets are a medium very well suited to be a channel for communication. Instinctively a child can grasp that he or she is not the one to be blamed for the things a puppet is saying or how it behaves. The puppets are ideal when it comes to hidden pain and grief.

In a case study, Madge Bray used a hedgehog puppet with a small girl making it go into the different rooms of a doll's house. The child screamed when it went into the bedroom: 'You're not allowed in there.' The child then went on to tell her secret to the puppet about her father abusing her in the bedroom. The hedgehog showed disapproval. Madge Bray assured the little girl that the hedgehog would tell no one the secret. She needed to have this precious fantasy life with this puppet friend—just as Penny from *The Rescuers* had her Teddy. Madge Bray also told her that she herself would tell what had happened. The little girl was then given hope that someone in the real world could help. But a child under such stress needs to have his or her life in balance in terms of fantasy and grim reality.

Madge Bray refers to her work in a case about the rape of a little girl—by working through toys which she animated, the little girl was able to play through her experiences again but under her own control: 'It seems likely that one of the healing elements of what occurred was that she was able to "replay" parts of what had happened to her, this time as a victor, with the full backing of some very strong people, including a Mummy who was very, very cross with the naughty man.'

Bjorg Mykle described two instances when children played the part of protagonist—they invented the scenario for the therapist to act with the puppets. One little girl had had problems with her behaviour at school. After rejecting all types of media she asked the therapist for puppets, and chose a very neat-looking puppet for the therapist to operate for her. She said abusively to it: 'You're a mess, you should never have been born.' She then instructed the therapist what to do and say. After that, she then took the puppet herself and played out her anger and grief, telling her secret that her grandfather had abused her.

Section 4

Communication, language and literacy
Puppetry: the language of the imagination
Autism and the puppet
Puppet animation and the early years at
    school
Physical experience of language based on
    exploration and play
Watching, listening and speaking skills for
    everyone
Creative role-play and the personal voice
    through the puppet
The manipulation of simple materials to
    make puppets for animation
Integration and empowerment

Communication, language and literacy

An early experience I had using puppets in a special clinic was for very young language disordered children. I sat with puppets in the middle of a group of two to four-year-old children who were displaying extreme misery and confusion by screaming, having tantrums, wetting themselves, hurling themselves around. Puppets were the last things on their mind, and I did not have a clue what to do. But it serves as a reminder to me still that children without language do not have the order in their brain to communicate—it is not a simple matter of speech and literacy, but rather a deficit of all that precedes it in terms of the thought process.

As an occupational therapist said to me at the time, 'language is everything', and of course, verbal and non-verbal, it is, and one should beware of looking at language problems in terms of speech only.

How can puppets help a child to communicate? In the more extreme kind of case, but useful to consider, Mickey Aronoff talks about using puppets in hospital, and how the anxious child is beleaguered in the middle of paraphernalia which threatens pain and punishment. He or she badly needs to explore and play to develop ideas about the invasive procedures about to happen to his body. Puppets can deal with all this—they 'speak' for the 'frozen voice', as she so aptly describes it. Puppetry can carry all our fears in the form of a puppet character—and we can take that character through the unknown on our behalf.

Imagination

(To imagine the puppet
is alive and act as if
he is alive is an experience
to share)

the puppet can be a protective
mask, a veil; behind it we can
experience a freedom to express
ourselves...

(I hear you
<u>through</u> the
puppet)

(I speak
to you
<u>through</u>
the puppet)

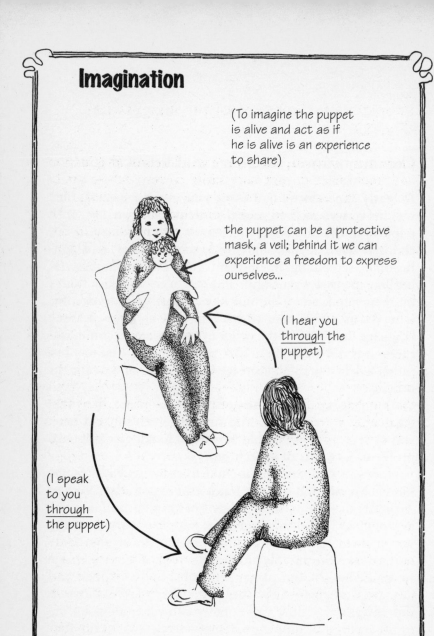

Fig. 53.

Puppetry: the language of the imagination (Fig. 53)

I have been very surprised at the way levels of imagination and intelligence do not necessarily correspond—particularly when performing to audiences with learning disabilities. The desire to make something apparently come to life before our very eyes is so deeply embedded in our humanity that it takes very little imagination for this to happen.

Performing in a ward for women with very severe learning disabilities, I heard a repeated scratching noise. It came from a woman lying under a table scraping her nails along the ridged surface of a radiator. Another woman sat rocking in a corner moaning to herself.

Gradually the group was brought out to me and, in the middle of them, I sang and told the story of the show with the puppets, without having any idea amidst groans and scratching whether or not I was getting through. I took out a tiny bird puppet—a ping-pong ball with a cardboard beak and bright yellow feathers on the end of a springy wire rod. On my other hand I had a little girl puppet. So I made the puppet hold out her hand to catch the bird and she gave it a kiss and stroked it gently.

Doubtfully, I asked the group who else would like to do the same. I was quite amazed when those apparently half-aware bodies unravelled hands from all over the place to appeal for the bird. I made the bird flutter around and land on each hand to be caressed and even kissed before fluttering on.

Some other examples also demonstrate how the amount of imagination required for puppets is much lower in relation to general intelligence than one might expect. They illustrate how the imagination has enormous power to affect what someone is able to do.

Language practice

John was fourteen when he came to me for some shadow puppetry sessions. He had severe learning disabilities with little speech and was almost totally incapacitated by muscular dystrophy. He could move his head a little and his fingers. With help he made a number of puppets and especially enjoyed a paper-puppet man on a spring that was made directly from his own painting—*'me'* he said (see Fig. 54). The most successful puppets, however, were a selection I made for him (on his direction) to use on the overhead projector. He initiated the activity by telling me what characters he wanted: he made attempts to say the words—*'Pleece, pleece!'* *'Gooh mah!'*, *'Bah Mah!'*, (police, good man, bad man).

I made a selection of simple paper and acetate puppets attached to drinking straws (see Fig. 55). I placed the projector on a low table, so that his hands were in line with the projector screen when they rested in his lap. He was able to shift his whole weight to get himself into the best position for using his fingers to operate the puppets. At times he would allow his body to drop far enough to allow him to use his teeth to grip with.

We projected the images on to the wall in front of us, and he enjoyed seeing them so large. The instant reward for his effort pleased him and encouraged him to work longer and longer at each session. His concentration increased from just a few minutes to over an hour.

He told me a long involved story about a man and his car. The car was stolen, the police went after the thief, then there was a fire and a fire-engine had to come. He had quite a good memory for sequence and kept repeating it, adding in detail and changing bits around to suit himself.

In order to perform his story to me, he moved the puppets around on the screen, became excited and moved them until they fell off the edge, then found another puppet or prop to continue.

Paper Rod Puppet

Fig. 54.

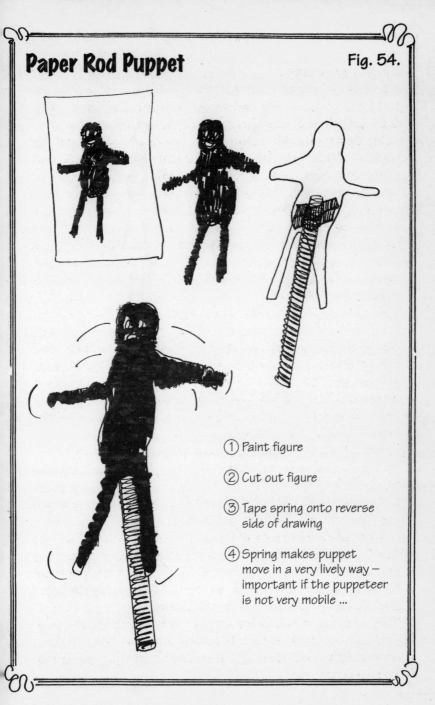

① Paint figure

② Cut out figure

③ Tape spring onto reverse side of drawing

④ Spring makes puppet move in a very lively way — important if the puppeteer is not very mobile ...

① Lay a sheet of clear
  acetate over white
  paper.
② Using special pens draw
  on the acetate.
③ Cut figure out in the
  way indicated.
④ Cut a strip of acetate
  and sellotape onto
  figure...

A Puppet for the Overhead Projector...

Fig. 55.

144

The very first time I asked John to tell a story he took a deep breath and then started to make a series of sounds in exactly the intonation one would use to repeat a tale to a child starting with 'Once upon a time' and ending with 'and they all lived happily ever after'. He used no words, just the tune of the tale. When he used words the tune disappeared and he struggled. He was an imaginative child who enjoyed watching performances and was now eager to perform to me. He enjoyed singing and would throw his head back and wordless sounds would come out in a lovely treble voice.

Puppetry offered him a way to use language, to repeat it and form sequences. It offered him a means to connect imaginatively with the ideas and things he was most interested in. I was surprised at the level of his ability to motivate himself to keep going.

Language and exploration

Sally was a large, ungainly eleven-year-old. She had severe learning disabilities, did not speak, and no one knew exactly how much language she had. She was referred to the clinic because she was refusing to walk. Some of the teachers in the special unit thought she might be regressing to attract attention as her mother had just had another child. My aim was to use puppets to help her learn more about how she was feeling.

I started off by asking her if she would like a story. She nodded excitedly because she had seen me using the puppets with other children. I devised a scene which included a new baby to see how Sally would react.

Mister Punch is asleep. He wakes up and calls for Judy as he is hungry. She has no time for him because she is busy with her new baby. Punch sulks, then in a fit of rage, collapses on the ground and refuses to get up again. He wants to crawl like a baby. Judy tells him not to be so silly, and then goes off to the shops, leaving the baby in Punch's care. Punch hits the baby and throws him away. A policeman comes along carrying the baby. He is cross with Punch and threatens to put him in prison unless he gets up and promises not to hurt the baby again. Punch promises. Judy returns and kisses Punch and they dance together.

The little performance at the table only lasted about five minutes, during which Sally's attention was completely held. She became so involved that, at the end of the story, she interrupted by standing up, pushed the table away and then danced on the spot with me (and the puppets). Usually she could be forced to her feet only by two helpers dragging her upright; on this occasion the initiative came from Sally herself.

Her reactions to the characters on the table in front of her demonstrated complete comprehension of the story. She recognised the wrongdoer and wanted him to change and be good. Sally particularly enjoyed displays of affection between Punch and Judy and would copy any puppet antics such as clapping and waving. She never spoke, but she made noises, pointed and waved one or both hands in excitement. She took each puppet in turn and rocked it— including the baby—and showed signs of wanting to be in the play. I started again:

Everyone is asleep. (Sally also pretended to be asleep holding on to the baby, so I included her). Punch is asleep, Sally is asleep, Judy is asleep. Who wakes up first? Sally pointed at Punch. She then put the baby down, picked up Judy and pushed Punch and Judy together for a kiss. Sally clapped in delight. She then gave the baby to Punch, pushed Judy away and fetched a policeman.

The play continued until Sally had had enough. This she showed quite abruptly by standing up, opening the door, going through, collapsing down on to her knees, and then crawling away. The following day she followed me to wherever I was working with the puppets. She was quite clear in her reactions to them. Her imagination was not stimulated by the ghost, devil or queen, but by the less fantastic figures that related more to her experience.

Puppetry enabled Sally to explore her own ideas about herself. They offered a playful opportunity for staff to understand her and to know how much she understood.

Whereas Sally was involved in quite personal play and performance was an extension to that play, the next example shows how performance can bring about change.

Peggy was a hemiplegic with mild learning disabilities as a result of being battered as a baby. When she was thirteen she was a puppeteer in our production of *The Ugly Duckling*. She had chosen to be a swan. At every rehearsal she put the puppet on to her bad hand, usually clutched useless at her side. It was doubtful that she would be able to lift up her hand high enough for the audience to see when it came to the performance.

The day of the show arrived. Everyone was very excited. I was backstage, behind the screen, pushing wheelchairs into place, when Peggy's teacher came round. 'Look, look at Peggy's arm.' The swan puppet was stretching and bowing its beautiful neck in a wonderfully graceful movement. Was it really that slow, clumsy, disabled teenager working that puppet? It was.

The excitement of performing for all those friends, who had come especially to see her, had overridden the paralysis for a very short time. There were people out there who were waiting for her story and she had the determination to bring it to life.

Puppetry and literacy

Claire was twelve with learning disabilities, and had some additional perceptual problems. She was diplegic with her legs being much more affected than her arms. Her hands were weak and shaky, especially when she made the effort to do anything requiring precision. She used a wheelchair but she could drag herself along the floor. Her class teacher wondered if a puppet might help her to concentrate better in her reading class, while her physiotherapist was hoping for a puppetry activity to improve her posture as she was tending to slide to one side.

In the home group she could help by laying the table, washing dishes and tidying up. She found difficulty relating to the other children and preferred to be alone listening to the radio. She had low self-esteem and she was not at all popular with the other children.

I asked Claire if she would like to help a puppet that was having trouble with her reading lessons. She was very eager to help, and proud for having been asked, which surprised me because, as she rarely played, rarely enjoyed the company of other children, I did not expect her interest in the puppet to be so strong. I wondered if she would have the imagination to sustain her interest during class time.

The class was at work when I arrived. As the children were all about twelve, I decided that I would not come in playing the puppeteer, but that I wanted them to feel that *they* were in control of the puppet—particularly Claire. I introduced the puppet, Hilary the Witch (see Fig. 56 and plates 15, 16, 21), to each child, and then, in return for their attention and at their request, I performed her as a puppet. The children were curious about her lack of a voice. I explained to them that puppets only have the voices that people give them and I praised them for asking the question. I made no attempt to make Hilary into a mystery—the children had to have control of the situation, as it would be their imaginations doing the work, their willingness to speak through

Hilary

Fig. 56.

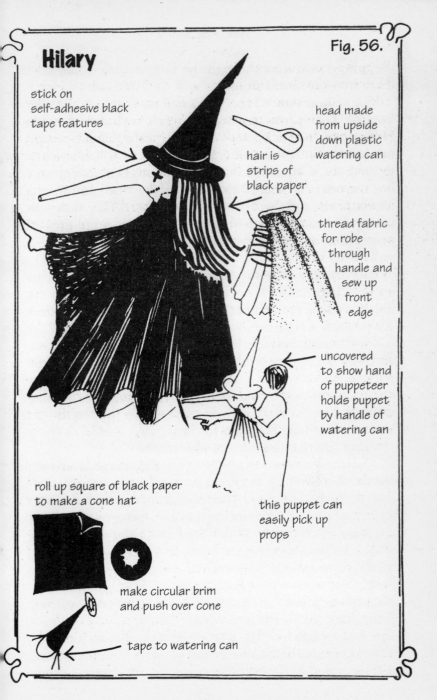

stick on
self-adhesive black
tape features

head made
from upside
down plastic
watering can

hair is
strips of
black paper

thread fabric
for robe
through
handle and
sew up
front
edge

uncovered
to show hand
of puppeteer
holds puppet
by handle of
watering can

roll up square of black paper
to make a cone hat

this puppet can
easily pick up
props

make circular brim
and push over cone

tape to watering can

149

the puppet and hear through the puppet that would take them into the world of magic and their reward.

In the meantime Claire was swelling visibly with pride because Hilary was coming to work with *her*! I made Hilary watch over Claire's shoulder as the child carried out her work. It was a literacy exercise in which she had to read out a word and then, out of a mass of letters, sort out the ones she needed to make up the word and fix the letters in the right order onto a peg board. The task was taxing her hand-eye co-ordination and her figure ground perception, as well as her ability to recognise words and individual letters.

Soon it was time for Hilary to take her share of the work. Claire took Hilary into her left hand and used the long point of the puppet's nose to point out the letters she needed. Claire was forced to use both hands (usually she only used her left hand for any task and then the whole of her body would slump to the right). Although the puppet was very light, it needed proper operating. Claire's posture improved as she used her right hand for sorting while she gave Hilary a voice to read out the words and letters as she held them up for her.

Claire played the part of the teacher as she 'helped' the puppet, concentrating easily for the whole hour-long lesson. She lived up to the obligation to play the part of helper, she had an easy, natural relationship with the puppet. She was so convincing in her 'performance' that another boy commented that he liked Hilary being there and he wanted to be next to work with her. It was exciting to see how easily Claire moved from fantasy back into reality and vice versa—showing a level of imagination previously unrealised. The puppet revealed a joy and creativity behind the shy, withdrawn child.

I used to think of the puppet as a *catalyst* to aid communication, but then realised the beauty of puppetry is the imagined personality of the puppet as subject to changes,

150

and as unpredictable as anyone depending upon what creative act is being worked by the operator. Then one day I met a student who referred to herself as being neutral when working the puppet. I can only say that although we play a game with the idea of the puppet being alive, like an autonomous creature, the link between puppeteer and puppet is never broken, and is in a continuous process of recreation in the responses of the operator and audience—neutral is not the word I would use.

To conclude:

- Puppetry is an accessible medium of communication for developing language by stimulating the imagination.
- The puppet enables one to communicate without fear, helping to alleviate the distress caused by a language deficit.
- The puppet is expressive with and without spoken language, but can encourage the development of both.
- The therapist, arts worker, puppeteer or teacher should set up means of introducing the puppet to the group and be able to evaluate what happens.

Autism and the puppet

It would be true to say that puppetry is *all* about communication, and we shall continue to explore it from that viewpoint throughout the book, but for now we shall look at some case studies which relate to the use of puppetry in a severe communication problem: that of autism.

Aileen Finlay, a puppeteer and storyteller who was working for the Scottish Society of Autistic Children, in a presentation she made to the London School of Puppetry, outlined three primary characteristics of autism:

- Impairment of social relationships: the children appear alone and aloof.
- Impairment of social communication: the children have problems with speech, or if they are verbal, they are echolalic (that is, they parrot what people say), they retreat from interaction—verbal or non-verbal—with others.
- Impairment of social understanding and imagination: this shows itself in a lack of make-believe, and play which is obsessive or absent.

On a number of occasions, the London School of Puppetry hosted Harborne School for autistic students in North London. These children who range in all ages were too severely disabled to go to mainstream schools. Visits to the London School of Puppetry were seen as a social occasion, and usually included making toast, finding out where the toilets were, playing with and making simple puppets, and watching very short performances by the puppetry students. A teacher commented: 'The management and the structure (of the session) were particularly appropriate—the "getting together" at the start in terms of introducing the workshops and your students.'

The young people were in the twelve to sixteen-year-old group. We showed very short pieces of performance—no more than five minutes each. The teacher commented: 'The various short sessions tested my students' attention span in terms of skills: sometimes watching; question and answer; creative "doing"; observing the performances; being the performer with their own puppets; looking at and exploring the different types of puppet; having to focus.'

All the performances were complete, not excerpts, and each performance was followed by a question and answer session to reinforce the simple cause and effect plots of the performances and evaluate the activity of the group as an audience. 'It was apparent at this stage that our students were interpreting the performances at their own level.' The teachers present were very pleased with this structure as it catered for the negative aspects of autism: inability to predict; conceptual and abstract understanding— behavioural problems and their inability to concentrate for long, and enabled them to build positively on to their social skills—in other words the performances gave a context for good behaviour, communication and comprehension. A teacher commented: 'I was impressed how my students managed themselves during the session, especially N who was calm and receptive in what could have been a difficult length of time. Even R seemed to manage to "hold" his attention for stretches'. Their own performance was a version of *The Wheels on The Bus*, a collaboration between Harborne and the LSP, and great fun. But best at the end of the morning was the triumph of loss of inhibition when a LSP student put some music on and everyone made his or her puppets dance behind the screen.

It was evident that through puppets and such a varied selection, that much learning can be delivered using a visual approach and supported by few words. The students have difficulties in understanding their own needs and emotions: through puppets their attention seems more 'caught' and 'kept'.

As a group activity, the event was exciting and unusual because of the amount of group awareness achieved, but Aileen Finlay in one of her workshops felt that she could not rely on the social cohesiveness in the group, as you might normally be able to do with children without autism. After setting up an attractive workshop corner on a summer play scheme, she set to work making puppets herself— and had others which needed finishing off. It was important to her that these figures should not be seen as dolls, and the activity just another kind of craft activity, but that the puppets should be seen as objects for performance from the start.

Six of the twelve children from the group then took possession of the space at different times and performed, asking Aileen to watch as they operated and helped each other with stories. Notable results came from three boys. The first was a six-year-old who would not wear shoes, showed striking aloneness, with no speech or eye contact. He took two puppets into a corner and had them speak to each other in nonsense language but with recognisable speech patterns. He was exploring communication at his own level—with the puppets giving him the freedom to do so.

The second boy, who was seven, spoke in a timid whisper and avoided social contact with others in too boisterous games. However inside the puppet booth he played energetically with the other children, chose monsters and crocodiles and, if there were none left, he called any puppet a monster, and also spoke in a loud voice both when performing and when he marched around the hall summoning others to see their show.

The third example was a boy of four with no speech, who as a spectator became very excited, pointing and shouting. In fact Aileen noted that as an audience most of the children tended to become more vocal.

What was interesting about this project was Aileen Finlay's conviction in the puppet as a potent medium in its three aspects: the object being made for performance, the object being performed, and the object being watched. In the illustrations above, the sense of the process is clear.

In another illustration, Nicky, an autistic boy, was part of a holiday workshop with children from mainstream primary schools. The other children found this nine-year-old difficult to play with because he did not look at them properly or speak, so we worked in separate groups to start with—myself and Nicky and the others on their own, while we found out under what circumstances he would make contact with them.

We had particular aims:

- To enable Nicky to complete jobs throughout the day.
- To encourage him to play co-operatively with other children.
- To have fun.

The class started for most of the group at ten a.m. and after our planning meeting, Nicky would be left at the door by his mother. We allowed him to wander around the room looking at whatever interested him. The other children welcomed him by touching him in some way: hugging, kissing, or just a pat.

On the first day we took him out shopping to buy materials to make his rod puppet (see Fig. 57). Nicky paid for all these items in a detached uncomprehending manner. We bought whatever he showed the slightest interest in— even a glance would do for us to ask him to pick it up:

A wooden spoon
Some wooden washers
A wooden screw
Glue
A plastic pan scrub.

We went to a café and Nicky had a milk shake. He was agitated about drinking it, but eventually did so with a great deal of encouragement. The whole outing was an experience for him. He was preoccupied with it all day and on occasions produced whole sentences, beaming all over his face. 'Milk shake, milk shake,' and 'I had a milk shake,' and 'We went to a café'.

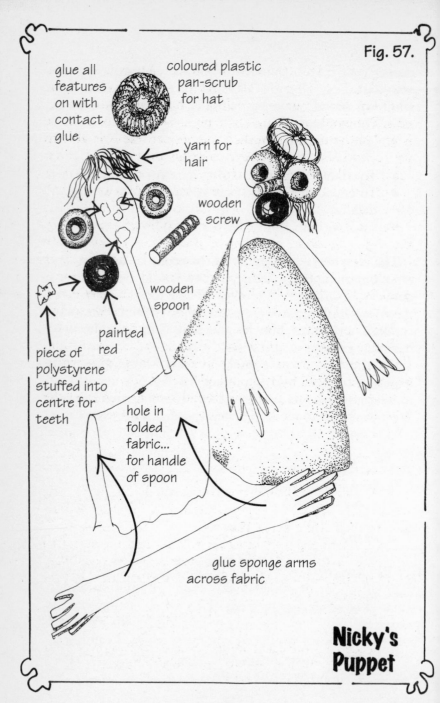

Fig. 57.

glue all features on with contact glue

coloured plastic pan-scrub for hat

yarn for hair

wooden screw

wooden spoon

painted red

piece of polystyrene stuffed into centre for teeth

hole in folded fabric... for handle of spoon

glue sponge arms across fabric

Nicky's Puppet

We started to make his rod puppet. He was made to select his own materials. He worked out how to locate the positions for features—developing his own body awareness. We would ask him where my nose is, where his nose is and so on until he finished the puppet. He was able to use scissors, but his hand-eye co-ordination was not good. He named his puppet Mr Nosey.

I performed my Punch and Judy show for the group and after that he asked me to help him to tell a story for Mr Nosey to act. He would tell his story himself after that to the other children. He enjoyed going in and out of my booth, playing with the zip, and jumping up and shouting hello to the other children. On that day Nicky had a loose tooth and that led to us playing a growling and biting game, and then the whole group talking about pet dogs, and from that Nicky made Whisky the dog puppet. He also made a Humpty Dumpty puppet out of a rugby ball and would sing the nursery rhyme from behind a screen, giggling when he saw Humpty bouncing (see plates 5 & 6).

In evaluating his work we found that he achieved the aims of the workshop. We did the usual evaluation:

1 *Q*. What kind of relationship does the little boy have with the puppet—is he engaged as a spectator or as a manipulator?
   A. Nicky was happy to operate the puppets and watch. He was quite mechanical in the way he performed while being watched.

2 *Q*. Once engaged in either role, is there a desire to give in to social expectations to respond sensitively and play along with what is communicated by the audience to the puppets and vice versa?
   A. Nicky understood that the puppet was for showing and started to enjoy the impact he made, but always needed encouragement to react to the audience—it was more or less on his terms at this stage.

3 Q. Is there a clear desire to use the puppet to communicate to spectators?

A. The puppet and associated things such as the booth seemed to be the only things that gave him a desire to communicate spontaneously.

4 Q. Is there the ability to distinguish between doll play that does not require an audience and puppet play that does?

A. Nicky showed no desire whatever to take his puppets home—where presumably they would become dolls and not be performed.

5 Q. Are puppets being used to extend social repertoire in terms of communication, intellectual content, expression of feelings, making moral choices?

A. He did start using the puppet to communicate to the other children.

6 Q. How appropriate is the action for the character depicted by the puppet?

A. He was able to relate specific action with specific puppets, particularly Whisky the dog and Humpty Dumpty.

7 Q. Is your client able to play jokes with the puppets—to play with the ridiculous, the unexpected?

A. He did seem to start to joke—especially with his jumping up and down inside the booth and using a funny voice. He also named Mr Nosey for his nose.

Nicky's family was enthusiastic about the changes it saw in him during the week-long workshop. They said he was no longer a shadow but a real 'presence'. He was lively, more adventurous, he was able to complete work and showed pleasure that he had made something.

Puppet animation and the early years at school

Whether you are working with children with disabilities or mainstream children in the earliest stages of education, the children can achieve the following with puppets:

- a physical experience of language based on exploration and play
- confident watching, listening and speaking skills for everyone, whatever their level of potential
- the ability to use creative role-play with puppet characters to express personal feelings and to identify with the feelings of others
- the manipulation of simple materials to create images and objects for animation
- integration and empowerment within the class group.

When I designed this project, it was after working for a day with teachers, who were concerned not about art or puppetry but creative writing. My experience in special needs has taught me that literacy is the end of the process of language experience, and the richer the experience of language the more chance of literacy.

It was also important to me to make a project that was appropriate to the way young children learn with their bodies. My aim was to create a project, which, after starting with me as a puppeteer, I estimated would take one day of training for both children and teachers together, and that the class would be able to continue exploring puppets and story-making together.

Physical experience of language based on exploration and play

One very delightful thing about working with very young children is their sheer physicality when it comes to expressing themselves. Their world is founded upon physical exploration. And most young children are 'hands on' busy creatures. Puppetry is a very physical activity and ideal for this age group with some provisos, however:

- A substantial amount of time should be spent watching the teacher or classroom assistant working the puppets.
- Projects should be organised so that the teacher and children are performing together, as young children do not have the organisational skills to hold a structure together.

A fragment of a story I use with young children which you might adapt as a model for your own material is given on the following page.

An ideal method of working would be to narrate a story that also includes stage directions. What I mean by stage direction are words that imply direction and storytelling action. Without this kind of instruction the children start to get silly and bash around with the puppets. This work will teach them to listen in an active way appropriate for their age and development, and they will enjoy the story because it is full of action.

Another important reason for working in this way is that young children should never rehearse repeatedly. The idea of perfecting something is an adult concept and actually take puppetry away from its roots in play where the children naturally are. The puppets for the story should be available for a period of free play without adult super-

160

In a wood there grew a tree. It started very small from a seed and got bigger and bigger. Its branches stretched higher and higher. And everything in the forest froze like ice.	Note that this is in the past tense because it is setting the scene. You need to place the emphasis on action words so that the children operating the 'tree' puppet can follow what you are saying. You need to have a device to freeze the picture the children have made before moving on to totally contrasting action.
The sun rises and is shining. The little boy crouches low down. One, two, three and jumps up as high as he can. He skips and hops because he is happy. He looks up and down and all around him. *Then suddenly he stops and everything in the forest freezes like ice because the boy sees the tree. He looks at the tree, he cannot move any more because he is so frightened.*	The sun can be a puppet and have its own scene. We now move into the present tense because theatre works in the present, in the here and now with the story unravelling before our very eyes. Show the contrast between happiness and fear.

vision. When it comes to performing you simply need to choose who is playing each role and narrate the story for an audience to watch. Shows should last minutes.

Below, I suggest a way of organising puppetry as a *regular* classroom activity. When creating your stories, you need very few—perhaps two per term—because with puppets the stories can be retold and retold. It is not just the plot that holds the child but also the characters who will become more and more detailed as the children get to know them and become increasingly inventive.

Exercise

1 Divide up the class into puppetry groups (perhaps numbered or colours).
2 Make a collection of puppets, mainly rod, which represent the variety of characters from the stories you want to cover. Ideally, it is better to have puppets made by adults because they last longer.
3 Take each group and tell them the story.
4 Leave them to play with the puppets freely.
5 Tell the story with the children acting the puppets and the rest of the class watching.

It is not necessary to build a special puppet theatre. But if the children want to hide, then simply push a table over on to its side, and let the children crouch or sit behind it. The legs of the table need to point out towards the audience. However, it is better that they stand to work because their puppet movement will be better. I use a wardrobe rail and make that into a stage (see Fig. 35). But there is no need to make it an issue. Most children play naturally with puppets, moving in and out of fantasy with ease, and the idea of needing to hide is something they learn from adults or older children.

Watching, listening and speaking skills for everyone

Regular playing and performing with puppets will have a marked effect on all aspects of literacy whatever the potential of the child. See plate 8 for storytelling with puppets.

Watching and listening as they become the story

Exercise

1 Working with a small group of three or four children, give them some puppets and ask the rest of the class to sit on the mat and watch.

2 Narrate the story very slowly, putting in plenty of action words and phrases. Avoid using description of surroundings. For example, rather than say *'it was a lovely day'*, say *'the sun was shining'* because it means that the sun can be a big smily puppet character. Rather than say *'it was a miserable cloudy day'*, say *'a miserable cloud floated across the face of the sun'*, then you have the contrast between the happy sun and the sad or cross cloud—two puppet characters. You might find it useful to go through familiar stories and adapt them in this way for puppet animation.

3 As you narrate, give time for the child working the puppet to react with the puppet. They have to listen hard and then find the appropriate action with the puppet. It might be necessary to add in some extra information. For example, *'the little boy is frightened and walks along slowly looking at his feet'*. You might know that the child in question, when worried, has a mysterious tummy-ache, or his head hurts—in which case you might change the narration to *'the little boy is very worried, his tummy hurts and his head hurts*

163

and he walks along very slowly', etc. Or perhaps, for another story you could add in '*Little Red Riding Hood is so happy, she skips along up and down because today is her birthday*'. As we all have birthdays, it will be much easier for the child to identify with the puppet and allow the puppet to become his or her surrogate. The other suggestion is to change the gender of characters freely—stories tend to have too many boys as heroes. Why not the Prince and the Pea? Or Cinderabba? Puppet stories can be *different*.

4 For yourself, try to identify issues that you might attach to the stories—which might enable children to develop their own perspective on social issues and make more recognisable puppet characters.

- A story about a disabled child who could not speak who was bullied by her friends (*The Little Mermaid*)
- A story about someone who was homeless and stole things (*Goldilocks*)
- A story about someone who was always late for everything (*Cinderella*)
- The story about a refugee who cannot speak the language of the new country (*The Little Mermaid*).

Listening to the story you narrate will be an enormous test for young minds, because they have to follow what you are saying and role-play it with the puppets. Once the children are used to the technique, you can have fun and change what you do without telling them—'*the little boy jumped up into the air and flew away like a bird*'. They soon start to listen, because they would not want to miss a joke. Watching and listening to what you are saying are vital skills, so the importance of this work cannot be emphasised enough. Remember to include an audience whenever you start to narrate, because they too will be attending very carefully to what you do.

This activity can work with *all* abilities because you can make their part of the narration very simple to start with—*the sun comes up*. They experience all the benefits of puppetry at their own speed of attainment.

Speaking

The children do not need to speak through the puppets when you are narrating, because it is more important that they develop the appropriate movement to match the vocabulary you use in the story. You will find that when you narrate the story (which you can change to suit yourself), they will be happy to leave the voices to you. As they get used to what you are saying and follow the pattern, they will want to join in—usually in unison. Use plenty of simple repetition such as Three Little Pigs; Little Ducks Swimming in the Water; The Wise Man Built His House Upon The Rock.

But little children love puppets to talk and want to talk back to them. When they play unsupervised, they will talk through or to them completely spontaneously. A little boy of nearly three with almost no speech, but who made appropriate noises without words, was working with me and watching what other children were doing. As soon as the word 'star' was mentioned, he broke into a complete rendering of 'twinkle twinkle' directed at the puppets— which we all recognised because of the movement he was doing with it.

Another colleague, who was performing for three-year-olds, had his plot interrupted when a child suddenly started telling the puppets about his mother's new washing machine.

You might need some more individual adult/child work with any child with behavioural problems—see any of the case studies—but they should still have the opportunity to perform to an audience—even if it is a very short moment of puppetry.

Creative role-play and the personal voice through the puppet

Allowing children to play alone with puppets is an important time for them, because it is then that they rehearse the 'possible' and try out relationships freely. If possible, keep an eye on them so that you can assess their interpersonal skills, or else set up a video camera to watch their play later. It does not matter if they know the camera is there, and they might enjoy watching themselves on a rainy day—but it can be very boring for you as well as thoroughly entertaining. Take up some of the ideas you see them come up with, and put the issues into familiar stories. You might try *hot seating* a puppet. This is a familiar drama exercise.

Exercise

1 You or another adult need to be fully and equally participating and be the first to do the exercise.
2 Simply take a puppet and sit it down in full view of the group. When a child has her turn to operate she may prefer to be hidden with the puppet only visible to the audience.
3 Allow the children in the group to ask the puppet any questions they like. For example, *What do you like for breakfast?* Perhaps limit it to five questions to start with.
4 The puppet answers in character.

Section 4

The manipulation of simple materials to make puppets for animation

Although you might enjoy a puppet-making session, sometimes it is a good idea to make puppets very quickly and spontaneously and throw them away after the game. Anything can be used to make a puppet. You might put potatoes on to sticks and give them felt-tip faces, or make puppets out of paper plates. You could put self-adhesive eyes on to objects—there are endless ways of making puppets. But it must be remembered that they are not dollies but objects being made for a purpose—*for animation*. In my own workshops for schools, when working with the very young, I do something very special—I enable the children to bring their classroom to life by putting eyes, noses and mouths on to the furniture and toys, and then we tell each other a 'something went bump in the night story'. When we had thrown the puppets away, one child came to me and said that it was brilliant, he wanted to do it again and again and again. Another child told me that her puppet was still in her imagination, even though it was thrown away. In her therapeutic work, Madge Bray uses a wide range of toys for young children to play with and bring to life. She skilfully enables children to animate by working alongside them, asking questions and drawing them into games.

Integration and empowerment

Every child deserves his or her place within the group. And the miserable experience of young children trying to achieve this in the face of bullying from the moment they start school until they leave at the earliest possible moment shows how important this is. Puppetry can enable children to find their place, because as we have seen in other parts of this book, the puppet enables the child to explore issues in safety. Weaker children can be empowered in that they can say what they feel. Every issue affecting children can be explored in puppetry.

After some training with the London School of Puppetry, the Over the Top Puppet Company ran a special two-week infant/nursery project on bullying with nearly 300 children. The children linked the puppet-making and performing with stories which shared the anti-bullying focus: Billy Goats Gruff, Three Little Pigs, The Ugly Duckling and Prince Cinders. The project reinforced their thinking about the issue of bullying in a very positive way. And in the evaluation it was mentioned that the children had introduced the idea of 'hugging'.

The head teacher noted the benefits to every child in the development of speaking and listening skills, art and technology and, in addition, the positive attitudes shown by quiet and reserved children. The teachers had developed in confidence and skills to be able to use puppets in the classroom themselves.

Section 5

I am the story
Losing control
The audience, and what takes place there

I am the story

I do not think there is anything more moving to me than seeing comprehension dawn in the eyes of someone for whom it has been a day-long struggle to understand for themselves. When working with people with learning disabilities it is easy to become too directive and fail to allow enough time for ideas—albeit in very slow minds—to grow and flower. As visiting artists we are forced to offer workshops in which there is a large amount of activity and product, but on only one occasion in all of my professional life have I been asked to work very slowly, and that was for the excellent Goldhay Group in Peterborough.

I have encountered some very negative attitudes to puppetry, in particular from care workers and social workers working with adults with learning disabilities. In general, the criticisms have been that puppets and fantasy are babyish and that asking an adult (and especially someone with a disability) to be involved is to show them a lack of respect. Although such assertions demonstrate a somewhat limited view of puppetry, some years ago I decided to question my practice and explore puppetry afresh, keeping these workers in mind. I was interested in work that:

- provided a medium that could be both fluid and yet quite figurative if necessary, but not doll-like
- used images that need not be interpreted as babyish or immature but would suit adults of all kinds
- did not depend on elaborate puppet-making.

I decided to do a simpler version of a project called *Shadow House* which I started with London School of Puppetry students and which they have taken as far afield as Romania, Israel and Ireland.

The original *Shadow House* was a site-specific installation using ropes, step ladders, bamboo canes, many different kinds of material to make the sides of a huge tent—polythene, silks, cottons, muslin, sheeting, lace curtains—anything we could get our hands on, in fact. We would spend a day building tunnels, and inner rooms, great chambers, and then, having made it, put in different kinds of light sources: reading lamps, theatre lights on dimmers, overhead projectors, torches.

Then we explored the different surfaces with shadow puppets that slid and jumped and crept around in the Shadow House, telling stories involving space and location in unusual and stimulating ways. Puppeteers move invisibly and silently from space to space, out of sight of the audience, creating magical images like unseen servants.

The audiences of other students or invited school children (usually on poetry projects) would encounter these stories as they explored the spaces of the House, or sometimes, as they crawled through a tunnel, the images would appear on the tunnel walls, or in the great chambers they would lie on their backs and listen to immense sweeps of music as images washed over them.

The *Shadow House* is an exciting project we have repeated many times. But it is also a large project needing several puppeteers to be truly effective. See photo plates 2 & 3.

For the special needs day in question, I decided to try out a simpler version, using just one very large screen, two theatre lights on stands, an overhead projector, and several halogen torches and various objects for projection.

Before the workshop started I put up the huge drape made of a very pale artificial silk. We were working in an actual theatre space with total blackout. I did not take any puppets at all but took some very simple materials for making some puppets and a colour wheel (see Fig. 25).

I had been asked to use *Warchild* as the theme for the workshop. It is a music theatre piece about children fleeing from persecution in the war, and the National Youth Music Theatre was performing it in the city the following week. The workshops were to prepare audiences and develop interest and knowledge of the piece. With my special needs group, and reflecting on the problems a social worker leader of my past experience had had with fantasy, I decided to keep off the mythic aspects in the *Warchild* story, which involved a Mermaid and a Prince, and, instead, try to put each individual into the position of having a home and it being assaulted in some way. The idea of the house seemed an everyday kind of thing, easy for everyone to relate to.

The workshop started with the group of about fifteen adults coming into the space—two of them had already helped me to put up the screen. This screen was approximately 17 metres square. It dropped about 8 metres, leaving a lot of spare rolled up on the floor below. The work went as follows:

We all made some rough human figures using torn paper. We used some pieces of withy to make rods. I also asked the group to name their figures—with their own names or any other.

I then projected a house on to the screen and invited the group members to make their puppets enter the house and tell their particular story. It was at this point a man said to me with great dignity, '*I am the story*'.

We then made monsters that came to attack the house. The group decided how they could get rid of the monsters: with police, fire engines—which I cut out quickly as required. All this was a very relaxed session with group members, including helpers, all sitting on the floor together, helping each other and participating in the drama.

We then split the group and worked both sides of the screen. The monsters came from behind and the images made were enormous—perhaps three or four metres high—and for this we used the stage lights and a small dimmer pack.

After lunch, the group was quite tired, as the work was very intensive. I played some music and encouraged the group members to make shadows on the screen while the rest of us watched. Sometimes they held torches from well back behind the screen and showed up the shadows of their colleagues—out at the front we guessed who they were. Those who were the shadows began to realise quite slowly that *they* were the shadows. In fact as I watched them, they all began to have some realisation of the images they were making. A man with huge concentration discovered that the hand shape on the screen was *his* hand, that the red colour was from the gel he was holding.

The day ended with a shadow dance—everyone taking turns to watch. We unwrapped the spare ten metres of the screen and several of us billowed the cloth and made it leap and swell as if in a sea storm; the people danced and their shadows grew and shape-shifted, sometimes as small as a human being and then up into a bloated striding giant.

My reflections on the day drew me to the following conclusions:

- I had thought a day would be too long, but it was time the group needed to assimilate ideas and start to be creative.
- It is easy to think that a short session would be best, but what I learnt from this experience was that a day is the *minimum*, but that it needs to be split into various activities differing in pace.
- It is important to respond sensitively to what the group might have to say in their own ways, in order to create a rhythm to the day's work.

- Despite my attempt to keep the fantasy out of the work, it somehow got in, with the group relishing monsters devouring houses, playing with the most tantalising terrors.

The group then went on to make a show based on shadows and their fears, that they performed locally and at the Edinburgh Festival.

This group provided me with what I needed to re-think my work with people with learning disabilities. Using the medium of shadow puppets I have been able to put participants into storytelling in such a way that they become the story, and to a greater extent can tell something of themselves to an audience, using imagery to extend and elaborate on their self-image.

The problem I found was that most day centres where most adults with learning disabilities may be found do not have any large spaces with blackout available. I have put the Goldhay Group type workshop on hold for now and have developed a smaller version as follows.

Visiting Shipley Leisure Library I was put into a small room full of cushions that we piled up at one end. I hung the screen across the centre of the room, but it was clear that anyone in wheelchairs would be more or less stuck to the spot and anyone without wheelchairs would be hemmed in by the wheelchairs. There would be none of the free movement on both sides of the screen that was so rewarding for the Goldhay Group, but their access to theatre space was unusual. The other problem was that the session was only booked for one and a half hours. The question was not whether or not the cloth fitted, or whether mobility was being compromised, but, rather, could I or could I not set up a situation in which every individual could '*become their story*'?

The Centre staff were very confident about my visit. They had booked it many months before; they had heard of my work and felt it was appropriate. The group arrived with most of them mobile up to a point, and some with speech. The workshop was organised as follows:

- The first thing they had to do was make a torn paper figure of a person and to give it their own or another name.

- I then asked who would like to have the first story and someone said yes. I put their figure on to the overhead projector screen and they enjoyed the suddenly enlarged image.

- I added a balloon on a string to the character. I asked if she was ready for a journey. The storyteller said she was.

- On to the screen I put up a series of images—sun, sea, ship, car, etc.—and the storyteller said which she wanted, or, if there was no reply, I used what I thought was appropriate, and together we created the adventure.

- By using a range of images and movement—with the storyteller or on her behalf—the puppet had some quite hair-raising adventures, ending with a complete crisis.

- At this point, I told her she needed help and that she had to call someone to help her. This caused considerable mirth within the group, because it exposed boyfriend/girlfriend relationships not previously obvious. What was interesting to me was that even if the puppet figures did not have the name of their maker/operator, the group still regarded the puppet as the surrogate of its owner.

176

- The puppet that came to the rescue was then given the balloon, and the story ended with a dance. The puppets stayed on the screen and the participants danced with the shadows.
- One participant and helper spent the whole session watching from the other side of the screen.

Everyone who wanted to told their story—there was a very positive, intelligent response to the puppets. One young woman made it clear that no one in the group was going to rescue *her* and I had to make her a '*Mum Puppet*'. Later on she was very excited to be dancing with her '*Mum*'—she asked us to project her puppet to make an image large enough to partner on the screen. Another man would not make anything himself but gave very clear instructions to a helper to make him a horse shadow puppet—but he still wanted the same series of story images.

Most of the group needed help at every point of the making. But they could see quite clearly what each part of the process was—simply tearing out a shape of a person.

Questions and answers ('Do you want him to have a head?' 'Arms?' 'How many?' 'Legs?' 'How many?' 'Feet?' 'No?' 'No feet?' 'How will he walk then?' 'Shoes?' 'And feet?' 'OK'.) ensured that no helper took over, and that each person recognised their puppet.

Taking into account the length of the session available, and my own preparation, making some images for use on the screen was unavoidable, but I think these images might be developed to include everyday options like shopping, going to the club, going to Bingo etc. The theme of the workshop was *Best Friends*, but this could be anything—such as *Favourite Food* or *Healthy Eating*. The structure of the workshop ensured that everyone was fully engaged. Both of these examples of '*I am the story*'—depended very much on my own willingness to perform throughout.

> I am confident now that it is possible for people with
> severe learning disabilities to tell something of them-
> selves through puppets and particularly using shadow
> puppets.

Losing control

Whilst making the observation that choosing to use a transitional object is the first creative act of the infant, as the
baby seeks to replace the not-always-available breast with
an agreed substitute, such as the corner of a blanket, toy
or dummy, the infant makes his or her imaginative and
innovative journey from self-centredness through a dual-
istic-me-and-the-rest-of-the-world-conflict into social and
collaborative peace. The object has become a bridge
between the child and the outside world. This object is not
something passive and static, for just as the breast was
warm and responded physically to the touch of the baby,
the surrogate also has character, and, without prompting,
the carer makes it have voice and character movement,
which elicits response in the baby, or responds to the attention of the baby . . .

But I want to get quickly to my final question. If the
transitional object, this animated object, is so deeply
embedded into our experience of life, then why is it we
have problems over its use? Speaking at a conference in
France, I was shocked at the number of delegates working
in psychiatry who had stopped using puppets because they
were frightened by the strong positive reaction created in
their clients by the puppets. Another colleague working
with children in hospitals discovered how few play therapists use puppets. The London School of Puppetry conferences have been full of positive reports on the use of

puppets. This book is the result of highly motivated, highly professional and very enthusiastic dedication from many colleagues ... and yet ...

One reason I believe that therapists and other kinds of specialists have problems using them is that, just as in using any other creative medium, they feel unsure about their lack of control of a client, and what is going on inside them, because they simply do not know enough about how puppetry works: the psychology of puppetry. Nancy Cole, who worked for many years in Canada, gave this warning in her book *Lend Them A Hand*:

> It is important for the person directing these (puppetry) activities to be aware of the power of the puppet as a medium in eliciting extreme dramatic response ... The healthcare professional may be unaware of the power of puppetry as a medium, untrained in useful manipulation techniques, and the construction of dramatic content. There could be healing at his fingertips provided he has adequate training in puppetry. Attempting puppetry without training may prove baffling.

Possibly another reason is that puppetry is often seen as a technical means to another end and the results over-contrived and controlled. Meyer Contractor from India, an authority on the use of puppetry in education, comments that: 'There is danger that the arts may be used merely as a tool for teaching other subjects. In education their first function is to develop imagination, initiative and individual thinking.' The roots of puppetry in play preclude the wielding of authority from a teacher or therapist over the client or patient. We cannot force people to play. The only control we can exert is to prevent a person playing; and, in doing that, we cripple. There is such a thing as artistic conviction. Creative expression gives personal coherence to the individual, even when the relationship of the individual to the world is confused or apparently irrelevant. Artistic expression particularises who we are as individuals. By using the range of 'languages' available to us, we are able to present our ideas and convictions to others and form relationships in coherent concrete ways.

The manager of a centre once asked me if I could use puppets for teaching sex education to her clients with learning disabilities. I knew puppets would not have worked unless talking about sex was something that was done openly and that the clients had thoughts and feelings they wanted to express on the subject. The official attitude at the time was that for people with learning disabilities sex existed *outside* the framework of human relationships. But creative expression is only about human relationships.

Whether we choose an entry into puppetry through watching, performing or making, the *meaning* of what is being communicated is never on the surface of the puppet action, which consists of the collaboration of the minds of the maker, the performer and the audience. In other words, no one is in control of meaning. It does not originate in the operator, nor in the puppet maker, nor in the audience, but *in the simultaneous multiplicity of ideas, tensions and resolutions that happen at the puppet performance.*

I suggest that, as we started, therapists, teachers and members of the medical profession, in recognising the usefulness of puppetry, actively seek training to develop their knowledge and their ability to use puppets, and that we make better use of the professional puppeteers in our community who have an interest in working in this very special area of artistic life.

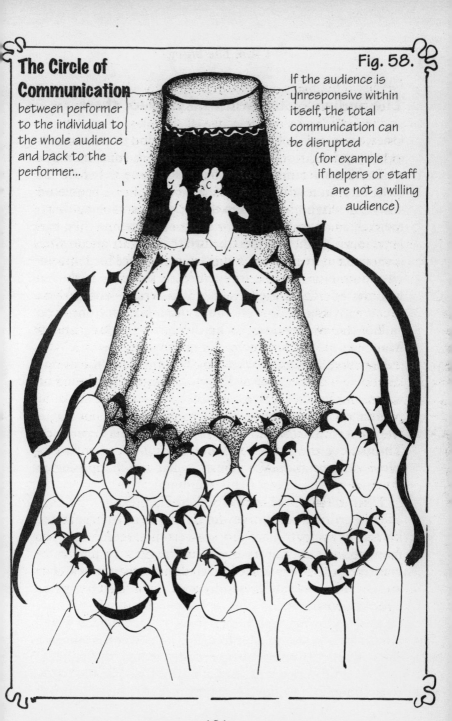

The Circle of Communication

between performer to the individual to the whole audience and back to the performer...

Fig. 58.

If the audience is unresponsive within itself, the total communication can be disrupted

(for example if helpers or staff are not a willing audience)

The audience, and what takes place there

Once, on a very hot day, I was performing in the grounds of a hospital. I noticed as I played that the audience was quiet. When I came out at the end I was greeted by the sight of a large group of elderly and confused people on seats and in wheelchairs. On the ground, or running down their chins or in their laps were the ice-creams they had been given by their helpers before they left to get on with something more exciting. Being in an audience for someone with disabilities can be frightening. If someone is shoved into the middle of a party, it is inhibiting—who do you speak to? Where do you look? And for someone who cannot get to the door, it hardly bears thinking about. Many people need support, it's not unusual.

Dorothy, a woman who was blind and with learning disabilities, came to see a shadow show. She depended on the reactions of all those around her—also severely or profoundly disabled. She sat listening intently. 'Lovely, it were lovely,' she murmured, wrapped up in the experience. Throughout the show the whole group had watched in silent concentration. Obviously, what was happening in the audience had been richly communicative.

What does happen in the audience?

The performance throws out hints of a reality suggested by the puppeteer. The puppets are the medium for the message. The spectators use their imaginative powers to construct the full picture in relation to themselves. The activity does not stop there, however. Each member of the audience communicates his or her experience to the other in an overflowing way rather than by a conscious 'I will tell the person sitting next to me'. The power to transpose the symbolic into the real experience through the imagination will be stronger in some than others; but the desire to communicate will override the disability, and that desire to share will draw a group together into a harmony, out of which healing in the social sense is available (see Fig. 58).

Lisa, a girl with severe learning disabilities and also heavily sedated, became so alert during the show that she responded to the performer by giving her name and, leaving her astonished teacher, went up close to the shadow screen to point at the moving image and said correctly, 'Bird'.

David came to a show with a few other children from his special school. His teachers kept their children away from the other naughty children from the mainstream school. Those children were getting all the things to do— and choosing and coming forward to join in. As the puppets performed, gradually David gave up being 'good' and crept forward, away from his group, very slowly to get nearer the show. He was given a musical instrument to play to accompany the puppets and an incredible look of delight spread across his face as he discovered a demand that was about to be made of him and he waited for his cue.

Bibliography

BETTELHEIM, BRUNO (1988) *The Uses of Enchantment*. London: Penguin.

BINYON, HELEN (1966). *Puppetry Today*. London: Studio Vista.

BRAY, MADGE (1991). *Poppies on the Rubbish Heap*. Edinburgh: Canongate Press.

COLE, NANCY A. (1993). *Lend Them A Hand. Therapeutic Puppetry*.

CONTRACTOR, MEHER R. (1984). *Creative Drama and Puppetry in Education*. New Delhi: National Book Trust.

COPELAND, AARON (1952). *Music and Imagination*. London: New English Library.

GERITY, LANI ALAINE (1999) *Creativity and the Dissociative Patient*. London: Jessica Kingsley Publishers Ltd.

HUTCHEON, LINDA (1984). *A Theory of Parody*. London, New York: Methuen.

JENNINGS, SUE (1979). *Remedial Drama*. London: Pitman.

JURKOWSKI, HENRYK (1988). *Aspects of Puppet Theatre*. London: Puppet Centre Trust.

KOMINZ, LAURENCE R., LEVENSON, MARK (eds). (1990). *The Language of the Puppet*. Vancouver, Washington: Pacific Puppet Centre Press.

LABAN, R. (1971). *The Mastery of Movement*. London: Macdonald and Evans (3rd ed).

LINDQUIST, IVONNY (1977). *Therapy Through Play*. London: Arlington.

LONDON SCHOOL OF PUPPETRY (1994/95). *Conference Reports*. Ray DaSilva. See next page.

NAIK, MEENA (1998). *Puppetry Workshops for Children and Young People*. Mumbai: Arun Naik (private circulation only) contact London School of Puppetry.

NORDOFF, P., ROBBINS, C. (1971). *Therapy in Music for Handicapped Children*. London: Victor Gollancz.

PHILPOTT, A. R. (1977). *Puppets and Therapy*. Boston: Plays Inc.

PHILPOTT, V. (1975). *The Know How Book of Puppets*. London: Usborne Publishing Ltd.

PLANT, MARGARET, (1978). *Paul Klee: Figures and Faces*. London: Thames & Hudson.

SHERSHOW, SCOTT CUTLER (1995). *Puppets and Popular Culture*. Ithaca, New York: Cornell University.

SHERZER AND SHERZER (1987). *Humor and Comedy in Puppetry*. Ohio: Bowling Green State University.

SIMS, JUDY (1978). *Puppetry for Dreaming and Scheming*. Early Stages.

WILLIAMS, GERALDINE H., WOOD, MARY M. (1977). *Developmental Art Therapy*. University Perk Press.

WRIGHT, LYNDIE. (1988). *Puppets*. London: Watts.

Resources

Puppet Books from Ray DaSilva Puppet Books. 63 Kennedy Road, Bicester. OX6 8BE. UK. Tel/Fax +44(0)1869 24593 dasilva@puppetbooks.co.uk
www.puppetbooks.co.uk

Little Angel Marionette Theatre. Dagmar Terrace, London

N1. Tel +44(0)02 7226 1787. Regular shows in residence and touring throughout the year.

London School of Puppetry—short courses, Diploma, workshops, conferences. 2 Legard Road, London N5 1DE. Tel. +44(0)02 7359 7357.

MusicPlusCo. Tel 0127 984 2812. Collaborative work using dance, movement, drama, music, puppetry and visual art.

MoversMakersShakers Tel 01756 753 495. Collaborative work using puppets, visual art, movement, dance and percussion including African drumming.

Pieces of music written as music theatre are particularly good. Lin Marsh, who is published by Piper Publications, has written several music theatre works, which are ideal for children and which lend themselves to puppetry, including *Tom Hickathrift*. She also compiled *Songscape* for Faber & Faber.

Index

Plate. 7
A version of
Hilary the
witch as a
catalyst for
school work

Plate. 8
Storytelling with
rod puppets to
develop watching
and listening skills

Plate. 9
Monster puppet by
Bjorg Mykle

Plate. 10 Simple table top puppet

Plate. 11
Shadow puppets